Key Stage Two English

Set A
Reading Booklet

This booklet contains:
Keeping Fit
A Day of Surprises
Harry Houdini

Contents

Keeping Fit
A leaflet about exercise .... p. 4

A Day of Surprises
A story about a trip to London .... p. 6

Harry Houdini
A biography of Harry Houdini .... p. 9

Keeping Fit

Regular exercise is important in order to keep your body healthy. Exercise can help to maintain a healthy weight, increase overall strength, lift your mood and may even reduce the risk of diseases like heart disease.

The amount of time you should spend exercising each week depends on your age and the type of exercise you do. Children aged 5-18 should do an hour of mildly difficult exercise every day, as well as taking part in activities which develop strength at least three days per week. Adults under 65 should exercise for two-and-a-half hours a week and concentrate on building their strength at least twice every week.

So, how should you start exercising? Warming up before exercise is vital as it prepares your body for the demands of exercise. A good warm-up increases the blood flow to muscles, providing them with oxygen. It increases sweat production so your body can maintain its ideal temperature and, most importantly, it reduces the risk of muscle damage.

It's crucial to do a range of warm-up movements before exercising. To warm up your arms, hold your arms out to the side and rotate them in circles. Body twists are another common type of warm-up movement you could do. Stand with your legs shoulder-width apart and slowly twist your body to look to each side, keeping your feet completely still. To complete your warm-up, slowly bend forwards, keeping your arms outstretched, and get as close as you can to touching your toes!

Once you have warmed up, you can continue on to the workout itself. Try to include a mixture of aerobic, strength and flexibility exercises in your regular routine.

Many people enjoy taking part in aerobic exercise, which increases the strength of your heart and lungs and improves daily fitness. Some examples of aerobic exercises are walking, running, cycling, swimming and dancing. These exercises burn fat and are the most effective type of exercise for weight loss. Strength exercises, in contrast, target your muscles, helping to make them stronger or maintain their current strength. These exercises include lifting weights, press ups, rock climbing and gymnastics. Strength exercises also have the benefit of improving bone strength, which decreases the risk of osteoporosis — a condition where bones are weak and more likely to break.

Flexibility exercises increase how much your muscles and joints can move; for example, general stretching, yoga (pictured) and tai chi all improve overall flexibility. Practising flexibility exercises can prevent injuries caused when generally moving around or doing other types of exercise.

When you've finished exercising, it's really important to take 5–10 minutes to cool down. This will gradually help your body recover to its normal condition and prevent drops in blood pressure which could cause dizziness. Cooling down also helps to remove any lactic acid which has built up in your system. Lactic acid is produced by your body during some kinds of exercise; too much can make you feel sore or sick. Walking slowly or doing stretches are effective methods of cooling down.

A Day of Surprises

Emily was wide awake before her alarm clock had a chance to sound. She flung back her duvet, emblazoned with the face of singer Rosie Ambrose, leapt out of bed and was ready long before she heard the familiar grumblings of her dad getting up. Saturday was finally here — it was time for the secret surprise from her Auntie Jane that Emily had been promised as a "Happy Birthday" on her special day.

Auntie Jane hadn't actually said that they were going to meet Rosie Ambrose at London's Cityview Shopping Centre, but Emily was convinced that this had to be the "surprise" that her auntie had been hinting at mysteriously. There was no doubt that Emily admired her auntie — she always wore fashionable clothes, watched the funniest films and listened to the greatest music. Emily was restless and fidgety as she anticipated the ring of the doorbell.

As they made their way to the station, they passed under an over-sized poster of the star singer, promoting her new album. Rosie's face grinned broadly down at Emily; her right arm cradled her famous purple guitar. Emily beamed back. Auntie Jane walked on.

The fluorescent letters on the side of the train spelt out 'London Euston', and Emily heaved a sigh of relief as they nestled down into their seats. The train gathered momentum and soon they were hurtling towards London, and Emily was increasingly sure that they would then go straight to Cityview Shopping Centre. She could finally get the signature she'd craved for years! She hummed the memorable melody of Rosie's latest song as the fields and towns were reduced to a blur outside.

London was teeming with people and traffic. The city's distinctive black taxis swerved through the streets, and groups of people swarmed around like angry bees. Emily clung to her auntie as they dodged suitcases, handbags and small children on the city streets.

"Surprise!" exclaimed Auntie Jane after they'd been walking for a while. Emily looked up and was shocked to see not a shopping centre, as she had previously expected, but the soaring turrets of the Tower of London.

"I know you've been enjoying studying the Tudors at school, so I've booked us onto a tour of the Tower. This is where Queen Elizabeth I was imprisoned!" Emily tried to force a smile, which in fact looked more like a grimace. It wasn't that Auntie Jane was mistaken — the ghastly stories of the Tower's past had fascinated her, but they were no substitute for meeting her idol. As Emily dragged herself around the Tower, she attempted to show a genuine interest, but her mind was preoccupied with the chance she'd missed to meet Rosie.

At lunchtime, Emily poked and prodded at the pasta that she would normally have devoured without question. Auntie Jane decided that she needed to say something.

"You wouldn't have enjoyed it at Cityview — you would have queued for hours to see Rosie for just a few seconds. Don't worry — the Tower of London wasn't the real surprise!"

Auntie Jane would say no more, and Emily was left confused and intrigued. But she did rediscover the spring in her step as they spent the afternoon admiring the gigantic dinosaur fossils at the Natural History Museum.

The sky was darkening, and the famous red buses were blinking on their headlights when Auntie Jane directed Emily into what appeared to be an average-looking office block. Inside stood a lean man of about Auntie Jane's age wearing a crisp suit. She greeted him with a warm hug.

"Emily, this is Chris — an old friend. He's an executive music producer, and he works here, at Prince's Road Recording Studios." Climbing the stairs, Emily could feel her heart racing uncontrollably in her chest. She suspected that the best part of her day was yet to come. Chris opened the door of the studio and stepped aside to reveal the room's occupant.

"Surprise!" Auntie Jane's lips widened into a beaming smile. There, her signature purple guitar by her side, stood Rosie Ambrose.

"I'm just about to record a new song. Have a listen, and let me know what you think." Emily's face was a picture of delight as Rosie began her song.

"One! Two! One two three four!"

Harry Houdini

A young Harry Houdini

Born Erik Weisz in Hungary in 1874, Harry Houdini was the son of a rabbi — a Jewish religious leader. The family emigrated to the USA in 1878. The family wasn't well off, so Harry worked a variety of jobs to help support them, including shoe shining, delivering messages and making ties.

During his teenage years, Harry read a book about Robert Houdin, a renowned French magician. His story inspired Harry to adopt the stage name 'Harry Houdini', and he and a friend created their own magic act — 'The Brothers Houdini'. In 1893, Harry met Wilhelmina Beatrice Rahner (known as Bess), and in a mere three weeks they were married. Bess replaced Harry's magic partner, and their show was renamed 'The Houdinis'.

The pair toiled away with only modest success for a number of years. Then Houdini began to focus on escape artistry rather than magic, and it wasn't long before he rose to fame as a solo performer — King of Handcuffs — in 1899. He advertised his talents by escaping from handcuffs in local police stations, and his show was soon one of the most popular of the age.

The danger of Houdini's acts escalated in 1907 when he hurled himself, handcuffed, into a river. The following year, he introduced an act where he was trapped inside a metal tank full of water. He had to free himself from his restraints and escape the locked tank before running out of breath. Houdini also routinely wriggled out of straitjackets whilst suspended high in the air, dangling perilously by his feet. These were just a few of the shocking escapades which made Houdini one of the most famous men in the world.

Challenging members of the public to devise traps from which he would then escape was one of Houdini's favourite ways to attract publicity. One locksmith reportedly spent years creating a pair of 'unpickable' handcuffs; Houdini took just over an hour to escape them. Another famous stunt involved Houdini being imprisoned, his limbs bound, inside a dead 'sea monster' (a giant turtle).

In addition to his passion for magic, Houdini had many other interests. He was a keen lover of planes, as well as cinema — he starred in several films between 1901 and 1918. With the outbreak of World War One in 1914, Houdini put his skills to more practical use, teaching soldiers to escape bonds in the event of their capture by the enemy. In later life, he also spent much of his time attempting to disprove psychics who claimed powers such as the ability to communicate with the dead. Alongside all of this, Harry continued to entertain until his death — in his later years he survived being buried alive, and made an elephant disappear into thin air.

In 1926, Houdini died from complications with appendicitis, aged 52. There has been much speculation about the exact cause: it may have been a simple case of appendicitis; some suggest he was poisoned by disgruntled psychics; others blame a student who had punched him in the stomach a few days earlier. (Houdini had apparently claimed that he could take any blow if allowed time to brace for it. However, reports suggest that he was hit whilst unprepared.)

Whilst the exact cause of his death remains unknown, he has been mourned by many. He is remembered today as one of the greatest magicians who ever lived, and he has been honoured in several ways, including a special postage stamp and a star on the Hollywood Walk of Fame.

Houdini being lowered, head-first, into a tank of water.

Key Stage Two English

Set A
Reading

Answer Booklet
1 hour

First name	
Middle name	
Last name	
School	

Date of birth	Day	Month	Year	

Total marks

Exam Set EHEP27

Instructions

This booklet tests your **reading comprehension**. The test has different question types, which you will need to answer in different ways. Each question has a space for you to give your answer. This will show you the type of answer to give:

Short-answer questions: you'll get one or two lines to write your answer on, so just write a word, a short phrase or a single sentence.

Long-answer questions: you'll be given several lines to write your answer on. You should use full sentences and explain your answer in more detail, giving reasons for your opinion or using quotations from the reading text.

Other types of answer: for some questions, you do not have to write anything. Instead, you might have to tick the correct box, circle the right answer or draw lines to match up words. Read the questions carefully and they'll tell you what to do.

The maximum number of marks available is written next to each question.

Do not start until your teacher tells you to. Start on page 3 and work through the booklet until you are told to stop.

Read one text and answer the questions on it before moving on to the next text. Use your reading booklet whenever you need to.

When a question mentions a particular page of the reading booklet, look at that page to help you write your answer.

You will have **1 hour** to answer all the questions.

SECTION 1

These questions are about *Keeping Fit*

1 How long should a child over 5 exercise for each day?

_____

1 mark

2 How does the amount of exercise needed by children compare to the recommended exercise for an adult under 65?

_____

_____

1 mark

3 Look at the paragraph that begins *So, how should you start exercising?*

Find and **copy** a word from this paragraph that suggests that exercise can be tiring.

_____

1 mark

4 Give **one** benefit of warming up correctly.

_____

1 mark

Keeping Fit

5 Look at the paragraph that begins *It's crucial to do a range of warm-up movements...*

Which of the following best describes this paragraph?

Tick **one** box.

The importance of warming up ☐

How often you should warm up ☐

How to warm up correctly ☐

Why warming up is fun ☐

1 mark

6 Read each sentence and tick **one** box to show whether it is **true** or **false**.

	True	False
Doing exercise can make you feel happier.	☐	☐
Adults under 65 should do strength-building activities for two-and-a-half hours a week.	☐	☐
Warming up makes you sweat more.	☐	☐
You should move your feet around when you're doing body twists.	☐	☐

1 mark

Keeping Fit

7 Choose the best word or group of words to fit the sentences below, and circle your choice.

a) People who want to lose weight should do

| strength exercises. | aerobic exercises. | flexibility exercises. | balance exercises. |

1 mark

b) According to the text, a good way to prevent osteoporosis is

| swimming. | yoga. | rock climbing. | cycling. |

1 mark

c) According to the text, flexibility exercises can

| remove lactic acid. | increase bone strength. | make muscles sore. | reduce injuries. |

1 mark

8 Look at the first two paragraphs on page 5 from *Once you have warmed up...* to *...other types of exercise.*

Suggest **one** of the main ideas of these paragraphs.

_____

1 mark

Keeping Fit

9 Give **one** way of cooling down according to the text.

_____

1 mark

10 What would you expect to happen to someone who does a lot of intense exercise without warming up or cooling down?

Explain your answer by referring to the text.

_____

_____

_____

_____

2 marks

11 Why does the text start with information about warming up, move on to different types of exercise, and then finish with cooling down?

_____

_____

1 mark

SECTION 2

A Day of Surprises

These questions are about *A Day of Surprises*

12 Look at the paragraph that begins *Emily was wide awake...*

How can you tell that Emily is excited about her birthday surprise?

_____

_____

1 mark

13 On what day of the week is Emily's birthday?

_____

1 mark

14 Read the description of Auntie Jane in the second paragraph.

What impression does this paragraph give of her?

_____

_____

1 mark

A Day of Surprises

15 What does the word *nestled* suggest about how Emily and Auntie Jane sit on the train?

_____

_____

1 mark

16 *London was teeming with people and traffic.*

What does the word *teeming* suggest about London?

Tick **one** box.

It's noisy. ☐

It's frightening. ☐

It's huge. ☐

It's busy. ☐

1 mark

17 *...the ghastly stories of the Tower's past...*

What does the word *ghastly* suggest about the stories?

_____

1 mark

A Day of Surprises

18 How would you describe Emily's feelings when Auntie Jane takes her to the Tower of London?

Tick **one** answer.

amused but tired ☐ angry and upset ☐

grateful and interested ☐ disappointed but grateful ☐

1 mark

19 *Auntie Jane decided that she needed to say something.*

Why does Auntie Jane feel that she needs to speak up during lunch?

_____

_____

1 mark

20 Tick **two** methods of transport that Emily and Auntie Jane use during their trip to London.

walking ☐ bus ☐

taxi ☐ bicycle ☐

train ☐

1 mark

A Day of Surprises

21 What tells you that it is dusk when Auntie Jane and Emily go into the recording studios?

_____

1 mark

22 How can you tell that Emily is a big fan of Rosie Ambrose?

Use evidence from the text to support your answer.

_____

_____

_____

_____

2 marks

23 The word *signature* is used in two different ways in the text.

For each context, explain the meaning of the word.

Context	Meaning
...the **signature** she'd craved for years...	
...her **signature** purple guitar by her side...	

2 marks

A Day of Surprises

24 Put these things in the order they happened.
The first one has been done for you.

Emily hums one of Rosie Ambrose's songs.	☐
Emily meets one of Auntie Jane's friends.	☐
Emily admires a poster of Rosie Ambrose.	☐
Auntie Jane and Emily stop to have lunch.	☐
Auntie Jane promises Emily a birthday surprise.	1

1 mark

25 Look at pages 7 and 8. How do you think Emily felt during her trip to London?

Explain **two** ways she felt, using evidence from the text to support your answer.

_____
_____
_____
_____
_____
_____

3 marks

Harry Houdini

SECTION 3

These questions are about *Harry Houdini*

26 When did the Weisz family move to the USA?

_____
1 mark

27 What inspired Harry to become a magician?

_____
1 mark

28 **Find** and **copy** a word from page 10 which shows that Houdini and his wife were very hardworking.

_____
1 mark

29 Write **one** sentence to summarise what Houdini's life was like before he became an escape artist.

_____

_____
1 mark

Harry Houdini

30 *These were just a few of the shocking escapades which made Houdini one of the most famous men in the world.*

What does the word *escapades* mean?

Tick **one** box.

Daring acts ☐

Unpopular pranks ☐

Expensive schemes ☐

Shameful events ☐

1 mark

31 Houdini's acts were often described as dangerous.

Find and **copy** three words or phrases from the text which support this view.

1. _____

2. _____

3. _____

2 marks

32 *...Houdini being imprisoned, his limbs bound, inside a dead 'sea monster'...*

How does the word *monster* make the reader feel about Houdini's trick?

_____

_____

1 mark

33 Name **one** other interest Houdini had apart from escape artistry.

_____

1 mark

Harry Houdini

34 **Find** and **copy one** word that shows that people tried to guess the cause of Houdini's death.

_____

1 mark

35 ...*some suggest he was poisoned by disgruntled psychics...*

Why were the psychics disgruntled?

_____

_____

1 mark

36 Read each sentence and tick **one** box to show whether it is a **fact** or an **opinion**.

	Fact	Opinion
Houdini died because he was hit in the stomach.	☐	☐
Harry was a good actor.	☐	☐
There was a stamp which featured Harry Houdini.	☐	☐
Houdini wanted to help the war effort.	☐	☐

1 mark

37 What does the phrase *mourned by many* tell you about how people felt about Houdini?

_____

_____

1 mark

38 How can you tell that Harry Houdini had a great passion for magic and escape artistry?

Explain your answer using evidence from the text.

_____

_____

_____

_____

2 marks

39 Based on the text, how would you describe Houdini's character?

Support your answer with examples from the text.

3 marks

END OF TEST

[Blank Page]

Contents

The Wonderful Wizard of Oz
The story of a girl's journey to meet the Wizard of Oz .... p. 4

Earthquakes
A text about earthquakes and how to prepare for them .... p. 6

Talking Through Time
The history of different methods of communication .... p. 9

The Wonderful Wizard of Oz

Dorothy and her dog, Toto, have been transported to a magical land called Oz. They are on a journey to find the Wizard of Oz, in the hope that he can send them home. They encounter a Scarecrow on their way who has joined them.

When Dorothy awoke the sun was shining through the trees and Toto had long been out chasing birds around him and squirrels. She sat up and looked around her. There was the Scarecrow, still standing patiently in his corner, waiting for her.

"We must go and search for water," she said to him.

"Why do you want water?" he asked.

"To wash my face clean after the dust of the road, and to drink, so the dry bread will not stick in my throat."

"It must be inconvenient to be made of flesh," said the Scarecrow thoughtfully, "for you must sleep, and eat and drink. However, you have brains, and it is worth a lot of bother to be able to think properly."

They left the cottage and walked through the trees until they found a little spring of clear water, where Dorothy drank and bathed and ate her breakfast. When she had finished her meal, and was about to go back to the road of yellow brick, she was startled to hear a deep groan near by.

"What was that?" she asked timidly.

"I cannot imagine," replied the Scarecrow; "but we can go and see."

Just then another groan reached their ears, and the sound seemed to come from behind them. They turned and walked through the forest a few steps, when Dorothy discovered something shining in a ray of sunshine that fell between the trees. She ran to the place and then stopped short, with a little cry of surprise.

One of the big trees had been partly chopped through, and standing beside it, with an uplifted axe in his hands, was a man made entirely of tin. His head and arms and legs were jointed upon his body, but he stood perfectly motionless, as if he could not stir at all.

Dorothy looked at him in amazement, and so did the Scarecrow, while Toto barked sharply and made a snap at the tin legs, which hurt his teeth.

"Did you groan?" asked Dorothy.

"Yes," answered the tin man, "I did. I've been groaning for more than a year, and no one has ever heard me before or come to help me."

"What can I do for you?" she inquired softly, for she was moved by the sad voice in which the man spoke.

"Get an oil-can and oil my joints," he answered. "They are rusted so badly that I cannot move them at all; if I am well oiled I shall soon be all right again. You will find an oil-can on a shelf in my cottage."

Dorothy at once ran back to the cottage and found the oil-can, and then she returned and asked anxiously, "Where are your joints?"

"Oil my neck, first," replied the Tin Woodman. So she oiled it, and as it was quite badly rusted the Scarecrow took hold of the tin head and moved it gently from side to side until it worked freely, and then the man could turn it himself.

"Now oil the joints in my arms," he said. And Dorothy oiled them and the Scarecrow bent them carefully until they were quite free from rust and as good as new.

The Tin Woodman gave a sigh of satisfaction and lowered his axe, which he leaned against the tree.

"This is a great comfort," he said. "I have been holding that axe in the air ever since I rusted, and I'm glad to be able to put it down at last. Now, if you will oil the joints of my legs, I shall be all right once more."

So they oiled his legs until he could move them freely; and he thanked them again and again for his release, for he seemed a very polite creature, and very grateful.

"I might have stood there always if you had not come along," he said; "so you have certainly saved my life. How did you happen to be here?"

"We are on our way to the Emerald City to see the Great Oz," she answered, "and we stopped at your cottage to pass the night."

"Why do you wish to see Oz?" he asked.

"I want him to send me back to Kansas, and the Scarecrow wants him to put a few brains into his head," she replied.

The Tin Woodman appeared to think deeply for a moment. Then he said:

"Do you suppose Oz could give me a heart?"

"Why, I guess so," Dorothy answered. "It would be as easy as to give the Scarecrow brains."

An edited extract from *The Wonderful Wizard of Oz* by L. Frank Baum

Earthquakes

Each year across the world, millions of earthquakes cause the Earth to shake and shudder beneath us. Their severity is measured on the Richter scale, with most of them so low on the scale that we don't even notice they are happening. But every so often, a powerful earthquake strikes, leaving devastating damage and disruption in its wake.

Earthquakes are caused by movements of the Earth's surface. The outer layer of the Earth is composed of vast floating plates that interlink like pieces of a jigsaw puzzle. These plates are constantly moving at an average of a few centimetres each year. Sometimes when two neighbouring plates manoeuvre past each other, they get stuck. Pressure builds up and when the plates finally jerk free, the ground shakes: this bone-shaking phenomenon is an earthquake.

Earthquakes are most common along the edges of these shifting plates. The west coast of the USA is located at a plate edge, making it prone to earthquakes. One such earthquake, the Hector Mine Earthquake, occurred in 1999 in the Mojave Desert in southern California. Very few people live there, so fortunately it caused almost no damage.

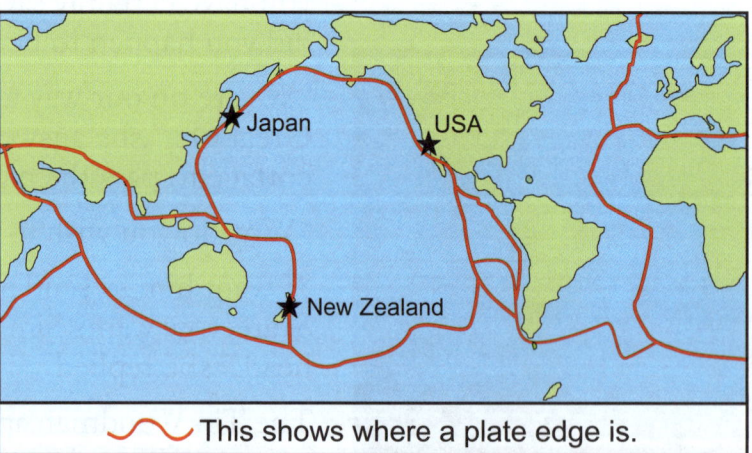

Japan, like the USA, is also situated at a plate boundary and, in 2011, suffered its most powerful earthquake since records began. It unleashed a tsunami (a huge ocean wave) that wreaked havoc in many coastal towns and villages. In the same year, the bustling city of Christchurch in New Zealand was hit by two powerful earthquakes just months apart. In an unfortunate turn of events, the second struck before there had been time to repair all the damage caused by the first earthquake.

Across the world, earthquake zones are not left empty and unoccupied; quite the opposite in fact. Many people live in places where earthquakes are a real threat. The work of specialised engineers and scientists is indispensable in these highly populated areas where earthquakes are common. Engineers have developed earthquake-resistant buildings like the US Bank Tower, which are designed to waver and wobble during an earthquake, but not actually collapse. Scientists also monitor common signs that an earthquake might be on its way, for example, changes in water levels and cracks in the ground. However these indicators don't appear before every earthquake, so scientists can't precisely predict the time or location of an earthquake.

The US Bank Tower

Fire from broken gas pipes

Homes in earthquake zones are often adapted to reduce earthquake damage. Heavy pieces of furniture can be secured with robust, flexible straps so they can move without falling and sticky putty can keep smaller objects from tumbling. Taller pieces of furniture like wardrobes can be fixed to the wall using metal brackets. Some recently built homes have flexible pipes which are less likely to break during an earthquake. This reduces the risk of fire following an earthquake, when gas from broken pipes can come into contact with a flame, with explosive results.

Many schools and businesses in earthquake zones hold regular earthquake drills to practise what they should do if there is a real emergency. A three-step approach is common: drop, cover and hold on. During an earthquake, you should drop to the floor and shield your head with your arms. Then, if possible, you should take cover under a table and hold on until the danger has passed. In Japan, 1st September is National Disaster Prevention Day, when all Japanese citizens practise these drills.

Another way that people prepare for earthquakes is to assemble an earthquake survival kit. Damage from earthquakes often prevents rescue services from reaching everyone affected immediately, so these survival kits should allow an individual to survive for a minimum of three days without outside help. They usually contain such vital supplies as bottled water, tinned foods and a tin opener. First aid kits are included to allow people to treat minor injuries at home because hospitals are normally stretched to their limits after an earthquake.

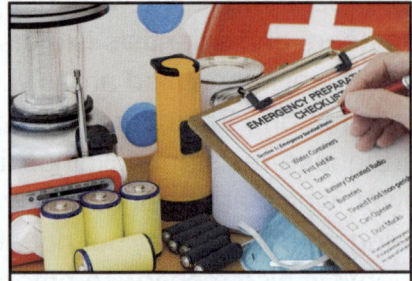
Earthquake survival kit

Electricity supplies can also be cut off by an earthquake, so a torch and spare batteries are essential; at best, the electricity supply is likely to be unpredictable. Dust masks and a whistle to signal for help are also useful — shouting when trapped can cause people to inhale large amounts of dust which is thrown up and lingers in the aftermath.

Damage after an earthquake

Although running is tempting, after a major earthquake, people should initially remain where they are as there may be aftershocks. These are smaller earthquakes which follow in the footsteps of the main earthquake, as the Earth's plates adjust to the movement.

When any aftershocks subside, uninjured people should tend to the wounded and inspect houses for signs of damage; if the damage is bad, people may need to be evacuated. At this point in time, the lengthy clean-up process can begin.

With so many earthquakes occurring with little or no warning, it is difficult for scientists to predict them accurately. This means that it is essential for people living within earthquake zones to be properly prepared.

Talking Through Time

Nowadays, we take for granted the ability to communicate instantly and easily with people across the globe. However, it hasn't always been so easy. Over the centuries, different methods of transmitting messages over long distances have been used.

The Royal Mail

The written word is one of man's oldest methods of long-distance communication. Throughout history, various ways of transporting letters have been attempted. The British postal service (later known as the Royal Mail) originated in 1512 with the appointment of Brian Tuke as 'Master of the Posts' — postmaster to the King himself. It was not until 1635 that this facility became available to the public at large. At that time, the price of postage was based on a combination of factors: how long the letter was and how far it had travelled. This expense was settled by the letter's recipient.

A Penny Black stamp

In the late 1700s, horse-drawn mail coaches replaced individual riders as the primary method of distributing mail. They were manned by a single, heavily armed mail guard. Another dramatic change occurred in 1837; now the letter's sender would be the one to foot the bill. Advance payment resulted in the introduction of the world's first postage stamp, the Penny Black, in 1840.

In the early 1900s, people started to send mail by plane, which made global correspondence much easier and quicker. The Royal Mail set up its first public overseas airmail service in 1919, flying between London and Paris. Since then, the British postal system has been modernised further — including the introduction of postcodes and computerised sorting machines. Mail is now transported by train, plane and van across the entire globe.

Telegraphs & Telephones

The harnessing of a new technology, electricity, was a major turning point for communication in the mid-1800s. Different ways of sending messages through wires were invented, including electric telegraphs. Pulses of electricity were transmitted from one device to another, which caused the second device to mark a piece of paper. The resulting messages — telegrams — were incredibly popular as they allowed rapid global contact between people, including journalists, soldiers and families sharing important news.

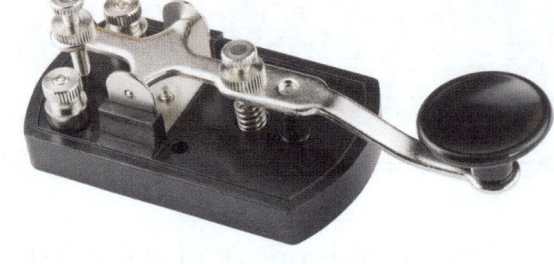
An electric telegraph

A rotary telephone

Alexander Graham Bell was exploring techniques to improve telegraphs when he began to investigate how to transmit speech electronically through wires. Simultaneously, others around the world were working on similar projects, and the official inventor of the telephone remains a matter of debate. The first telephone line in America was completed in 1877 and within three years the number of telephones in the USA was approaching 48,000. Early telephones were sold in pairs, connected by a long wire. In 1889, an automatic switchboard was invented, so users could choose who they wanted to call and the wires would be connected accordingly.

The next major advance for telephone technology was the invention of the mobile phone. Mobile devices that could make phone calls were first available to the public in 1984, costing over £2500 in today's money.

Email

An early PC

Before the advent of the personal computer (PC) in the 1970s, computers were unwieldy, expensive contraptions used exclusively by corporations and universities. As PCs became more commonplace in the following decades, people sought ways to use them to communicate with each other. It is generally accepted that electronic mail, or email, was invented by Ray Tomlinson in 1972.

His innovation was a program which allowed communication between two computers connected to the same network. Since this ground-breaking discovery, computers have changed rapidly, almost beyond recognition, and internet use has exploded. Now emails containing not only text but all kinds of media can be sent between any number of computers connected to the internet — the world's largest network.

Nowadays, many people use their mobile phones to send and receive emails in the blink of an eye. This is thanks to a new generation of mobile phones: smartphones. These popular, hugely powerful devices can connect to the internet, play videos and much more.

Throughout time, humans have endeavoured to find ways to quickly communicate with each other. With the advances of modern technology, our search seems to finally be over.

Key Stage Two English

Set B
Reading

Answer Booklet
1 hour

First name	
Middle name	
Last name	
School	

Date of birth	Day		Month		Year	

Total marks

Exam Set EHEP27

Instructions

This booklet tests your **reading comprehension**. The test has different question types, which you will need to answer in different ways. Each question has a space for you to give your answer. This will show you the type of answer to give:

Short-answer questions: you'll get one or two lines to write your answer on, so just write a word, a short phrase or a single sentence.

Long-answer questions: you'll be given several lines to write your answer on. You should use full sentences and explain your answer in more detail, giving reasons for your opinion or using quotations from the reading text.

Other types of answer: for some questions, you do not have to write anything. Instead, you might have to tick the correct box, circle the right answer or draw lines to match up words. Read the questions carefully and they'll tell you what to do.

The maximum number of marks available is written next to each question.

Do not start until your teacher tells you to. Start on page 3 and work through the booklet until you are told to stop.

Read one text and answer the questions on it before moving on to the next text. Use your reading booklet whenever you need to.

When a question mentions a particular page of the reading booklet, look at that page to help you write your answer.

You will have **1 hour** to answer all the questions.

The Wonderful Wizard of Oz

SECTION 1

These questions are about *The Wonderful Wizard of Oz*

1 Where is Dorothy at the beginning of the text?

Tick **one** box.

under a tree ☐

in a cottage ☐

by a river ☐

on the yellow brick road ☐

1 mark

2 *"It must be inconvenient to be made of flesh," said the Scarecrow...*

What does the word *inconvenient* mean in the sentence above?

Tick **one** box.

boring ☐

troublesome ☐

tiring ☐

complicated ☐

1 mark

3 *"What was that?" she asked timidly.*

How does the word *timidly* make the reader feel about the source of the noise?

_____

_____

1 mark

The Wonderful Wizard of Oz

4 ...*Toto barked sharply and made a snap at the tin legs...*

What does this suggest about Toto?

_____

1 mark

5 **Find** and **copy** a phrase which shows that Dorothy feels sorry for the Tin Woodman.

_____

1 mark

6 How do you know that the cottage belongs to the Tin Woodman?

_____

1 mark

7 *The Tin Woodman gave a sigh of satisfaction...*

Which of the following best matches the meaning of the word *satisfaction* in the sentence above?

Tick **one** box.

tiredness ☐

happiness ☐

pride ☐

gratitude ☐

1 mark

The Wonderful Wizard of Oz

8 How do you know that Dorothy has been a great help to the Tin Woodman?

_____

_____

1 mark

9 Put these events in the order they happen in the story. The first one has been done for you.

Dorothy oils the Tin Woodman's legs. ☐

Dorothy wakes up. [1]

Dorothy explains why she wants to see the Wizard. ☐

Toto bites the Tin Woodman. ☐

Dorothy washes in the spring. ☐

1 mark

10 Do you think Dorothy and the Scarecrow will let the Tin Woodman join them? Explain your answer using information from the text.

_____

_____

_____

2 marks

The Wonderful Wizard of Oz

11 Do you think Dorothy is brave? Tick **one** box.

Yes ☐   No ☐

Give reasons for your answer below.

_____

_____

_____

_____

2 marks

12 One of the main ideas of the story is that Oz is a magical place.

Explain how this is shown using information from the text.

_____

_____

_____

_____

_____

_____

_____

3 marks

Earthquakes

SECTION 2

These questions are about *Earthquakes*

13 What is the Richter scale?

_____

1 mark

14 How does comparing the Earth's plates to *pieces of a jigsaw puzzle* help the reader understand what the plates are like?

_____

_____

1 mark

15 Fill in the gaps in this table using information from the text.

Country	Year of earthquake
Japan	
	1999
New Zealand	

1 mark

Earthquakes

16 Give **one** reason why the Hector Mine Earthquake was less damaging than the 2011 earthquakes in Christchurch, New Zealand.

_____

_____

1 mark

17 *The work of specialised engineers and scientists is indispensable in these highly populated areas where earthquakes are common.*

What does the word *indispensable* mean in the sentence above?

Tick **one** box.

popular ☐

useful ☐

essential ☐

well-paid ☐

1 mark

18 Using information from the text, explain why scientists can't always predict an earthquake.

_____

_____

1 mark

Earthquakes

19 List **three** ways people can prepare their homes for an earthquake.

1. _____

2. _____

3. _____

2 marks

20 Why do you think there is a National Disaster Prevention Day in Japan?

_____

_____

1 mark

21 What would be an appropriate summary for the last two paragraphs on page 7?

Tick **one** box.

What causes earthquakes ☐

Why people should prepare for an earthquake ☐

Earthquake preparations ☐

What to do during an earthquake ☐

1 mark

Earthquakes

22 Briefly explain what you should do during and after an earthquake that occurs while you are at home.

_____

_____

_____

_____

2 marks

23 Why is using a torch as a light source after an earthquake safer than using matches and candles?

Explain your answer using information from the text.

_____

_____

1 mark

24 Why is it important to have a dust mask in an earthquake survival kit?

_____

_____

1 mark

Earthquakes

25 Do you think people should live in earthquake zones? Tick **one** box.

Yes ☐   No ☐

Explain your answer using information from the text.

[answer lines]

3 marks

Talking Through Time

SECTION 3

These questions are about *Talking Through Time*

26 Look at the beginning of page 9.

Draw lines to match each word on the left to a word on the right which could replace it in the text.

instantly		started
transporting		sending
originated		service
facility		rapidly

2 marks

27 Who was allowed to use the British postal system in 1550?

_____

1 mark

Talking Through Time

28 Choose the best word or group of words to fit the sentences below, and circle your choice.

a) Postage was originally based on how long a letter was and

- how heavy it was.
- the day it was posted.
- how it was transported.
- how far it travelled.

1 mark

b) Before horse-drawn carts, mail was transported by

- individuals on horses.
- boat.
- armed guards.
- planes.

1 mark

c) The Penny Black stamp was introduced in

- 1837.
- 1838.
- 1840.
- 1841.

1 mark

d) Since 1900, the British postal service has been improved by the introduction of

- more postmen.
- postcodes.
- sorting offices.
- armed mail guards.

1 mark

29 Why is it uncertain who the inventor of the telephone was?

_____

1 mark

Talking Through Time

30 Read each sentence and tick **one** box to show whether it is **true** or **false**.

	True	False
In America, the first telephone line was completed in 1877.	☐	☐
By 1878, there were almost 48,000 telephones in America.	☐	☐
Early telephones were connected together in pairs by a long wire.	☐	☐
A switchboard to swap the wires was invented in 1895.	☐	☐

1 mark

31 Why do you think personal computers became more common?

_____

1 mark

32 Look at the paragraph that begins *His innovation was a program...*

What does the word *exploded* suggest about internet use?

_____

_____

1 mark

33 Why has the use of email increased as the internet has grown?

_____

_____

1 mark

34 How are smartphones different from early telephones?

_____

_____

_____

2 marks

35 On page 11, the text says people have *endeavoured to find ways to quickly communicate with each other.*

What does the word *endeavoured* mean in the sentence above?

_____

1 mark

36 How does the text in the box at the bottom of page 11 link back to the introduction?

_____

_____

1 mark

37 Read each sentence and tick **one** box to show whether it is a **fact** or an **opinion**.

	Fact	Opinion
Royal Mail sent the first public overseas airmail in the 1900s.	☐	☐
Telegrams are the best form of communication.	☐	☐
Mobile phones were first available to the public in 1984.	☐	☐
Personal computers were the most important invention of the 1900s.	☐	☐

1 mark

END OF TEST

[Blank Page]

Key Stage Two English

Set A
Grammar, Punctuation and Spelling

Paper 1: Questions
45 minutes

First name	
Middle name	
Last name	
School	
Date of birth	Day [ ] Month [ ] Year [ ]

Paper 2, the spelling task, is a pull-out section in the middle of the booklet.

Total marks [ ]

[Blank Page]

Instructions

This booklet tests your **grammar**, **vocabulary** and **punctuation**. The test has different question types, which you will need to answer in different ways. Each question has a space for you to give your answer. This will show you the type of answer to give:

Multiple-choice answers: you can answer these questions without writing any words. You might have to tick a box, circle a word or draw lines between different words. Read the instructions for each question carefully, as they will tell you what to do.

Short answers: these questions have a line or a box for your answer. This shows that you need to write something. It could be a word, a short phrase or a sentence.

There is a mark box next to each question. It tells you the maximum number of marks for that question.

Do not start until your teacher tells you to. Once you have started the test, work through the booklet until you are told to stop.

You will have 45 minutes to answer all the questions.

1 Read the sentences below.
Circle the words which need capital letters.

we decided to go on holiday to egypt. my sister karen used lots of sunscreen to avoid getting sunburnt, while i just sat in the shade.

1 mark

2 Draw a line to match each sentence with the most likely final punctuation mark. You can only use each punctuation mark **once**.

Sentence	Punctuation
Where did Farid go	?
William could come for lunch	!
What a brilliant performance that was	.

1 mark

3 Read the options below.
Tick the option which is punctuated correctly.

Tick **one** box.

I love to read, my favourite books are thrillers. ☐

I love to read. My favourite books are thrillers. ☐

I love to read my favourite books are thrillers. ☐

I love to read my favourite books. Are thrillers. ☐

1 mark

4 Read the sentence below.
Tick the word that is a **noun**.

Although the search was long and tiring, he never gave up hope.

Tick **one** box.

Although ☐

tiring ☐

gave ☐

hope ☐

1 mark

5 Read the sentence below.
Choose a **conjunction** from the box to fill each gap and write it on the line.
You can only use each conjunction **once**.

> as   unless   and

You can go to the shop _____ buy a DVD _____ you would

rather get a game. You can choose _____ it's your pocket money.

1 mark

6 Read the sentence below. In the box, write the **contracted form** of the words that are underlined.

Howie <u>will not</u> stop until he finds his missing slipper.

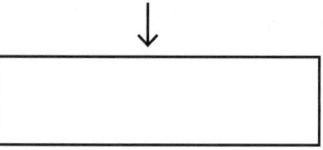

1 mark

7 Read the sentence below.
Write the **name** of the punctuation mark that appears between the words mess and it on the line.

I know who made the mess — it was my baby brother.

_____

1 mark

8 Look at the table below. Change the question into a **command**.
Write the command in the right-hand column.

Question	Command
Would you close the door?	

1 mark

9 Read the sentence below and circle the word or words that make it a **question**.

You can still take me swimming on Saturday, can't you?

1 mark

10 The sentence below is missing an **exclamation mark**.
Tick **one** box to show where the exclamation mark should go.

"I don't want to go to the museum" cried Seb.
↑   ↑   ↑   ↑
☐   ☐   ☐   ☐

1 mark

11 Read the sentence below.
Write what Colin needs as a list of bullet points below.
Make sure you use correct punctuation.

Colin needs to buy bread, butter, ham and cheese from the shop.

From the shop, Colin needs:

• _____

• _____

• _____

• _____

1 mark

12 Read the sentence below.
Tick the pair of **pronouns** that best completes the sentence.

I thought _____ presentation was even better than _____.

Tick **one** box.

his   me   ☐

he   mine   ☐

he   me   ☐

his   mine   ☐

1 mark

13 Look at the table below. Put a tick in each row to show whether each sentence is a **statement** or a **command**.

Sentence	Statement	Command
You must bring her some more food.		
Jameela asked for some more food.		
Go to the kitchen if you want more food.		

1 mark

14 Draw a line to match each word with its **antonym**.
You can only use each antonym **once**.

Word	Antonym
continuous	trust
doubt	delicate
robust	intermittent
conform	oppose

1 mark

15 Circle all the words in the sentence below that should have an **apostrophe**.

Shes lost Mums new bag. I dont know how she can be so careless.

1 mark

16 Look at the table below.
For each answer, write an appropriate question.

One has already been done for you.

Question	Answer
What is your favourite colour?	Purple.
	I love it!
	I go swimming.

1 mark

17 Complete the sentence below by filling in the gap with an appropriate **adverb**.

Pat whistled a tune _____ .

1 mark

18 Read the sentences below.
Circle all the **conjunctions**.

If we don't get home by seven, we'll be late for the film and Dad will be cross. We should hurry as it's already six o'clock.

19 Tick the box below the part of the sentence that is a **relative clause**.

Sally forgot | that the curry | which Jim had made | was still in the oven.

20 Read the sentence below. Put **V** in the box under the **verb**, **S** in the box under the **subject** and **O** in the box under the **object**.

Kirsten opened the door.
 ↑   ↑   ↑
 □   □   □

1 mark

21 Read the sentences below. Tick the **two** sentences which are **formal**.

Tick **two** boxes.

Kathryn has requested that we eat beef. □

Aaron likes beef, doesn't he? □

I can't believe how tasty this is. □

The dessert was equally delicious. □

1 mark

22 Read the sentences below. Change all the underlined verbs from the **present** tense to the **past** tense.

One has already been done for you.

| was |

↑

Before performances, I <u>am</u> very nervous.

[ ]

↑

The carrots <u>grow</u> in the vegetable patch.

[ ]

↑

Smruti <u>dislikes</u> cold weather.

[ ]

↑

After being stung, I <u>begin</u> to cry.

1 mark

23 Read the passage below. Write an **adjective** derived from the noun in brackets in each space. One has already been done for you.

Although horse riding can be __dangerous__ [danger], with good training you

can learn to ride safely. In my _____ [person] opinion, horses are

_____ [beauty] animals.

1 mark

Key Stage Two English

Set A
Grammar, Punctuation and Spelling

Paper 2: Spelling

First name	
Middle name	
Last name	
School	
Date of birth	Day Month Year

Total marks

Exam Set EHEP27

Spelling Test

1. The King of Spain is my _____ relative.

2. Be careful not to _____ your tickets.

3. Kate is driving, and Kofi is _____ her on his bike.

4. The door is _____ left unlocked.

5. They acted _____ to make a good impression.

6. Karine likes to _____ in other people's business.

7. Siân makes _____ cupcakes and biscuits.

8. The dancers felt more _____ after the rehearsal.

9. Many animals live in _____ groups.

10. Toads have _____ skin.

11. The storm is _____ with my radio.

12. We had a _____ examination before the dive trip.

13. He had to _____ a lot of free time to become a sprinter.

14. My mum's _____ just looks like a scribble.

15. The _____ statue sold for a lot of money.

16. Joe used to _____ the children with his juggling.

17. She is the most _____ person that I know.

18. You need to _____ spelling tricky words.

19. The weather always _____ my mood.

20. There is a _____ difference between the colours.

END OF TEST

[Blank Page]

24 Read the sentences below.
Tick the sentence which uses **brackets** correctly.

Tick **one** box.

My English teacher (Mrs Ferraz runs the local book club). ☐

My English teacher Mrs Ferraz runs the (local book club). ☐

My (English teacher) Mrs Ferraz runs the local book club. ☐

My English teacher (Mrs Ferraz) runs the local book club. ☐

1 mark

25 Draw lines to match each sentence with the correct **function**.
Each function box should only be used **once**.

Sentence	Function
What a scary lion we saw at the zoo	statement
Don't stand too close to the lion enclosure	question
What time will the lions be fed at the zoo	command
There are six lions and two cubs at this zoo	exclamation

1 mark

26 Read the sentence below.
Rewrite the sentence as **direct speech**. Make sure you use correct punctuation.

Samantha asked if he would like a new jumper.

Samantha asked him, _____

_____

1 mark

27 Read the sentences below.
Tick **one** box to show which sentence means you are **most likely** to go to the cinema tomorrow.

Tick **one** box.

I may go to the cinema tomorrow. ☐

I can go to the cinema tomorrow. ☐

I shall go to the cinema tomorrow. ☐

I might go to the cinema tomorrow. ☐

1 mark

28 Read the sentences below.
Tick the sentence which is written in the **active voice**.

Tick **one** box.

The delays were caused by a broken-down tractor. ☐

The farmer apologised for the delays. ☐

A meeting was called to discuss the problems. ☐

Several suggestions were proposed by local people. ☐

1 mark

29 Tick **one** box to show where the **hyphen** should go in this sentence.

We had lunch at a nice family owned café last weekend.

1 mark

30 Look at the table below. Put a tick in each row to show whether each **adverb** describes a time or a place.

Adverb	Time	Place
yesterday		
near		
rarely		
behind		

1 mark

31 Read the sentence below.
Tick **one** box to show what the word '**who**' is.

Finn plays cricket with a boy **who** plays for England.

Tick **one** box.

a possessive adjective ☐

a determiner ☐

a noun ☐

a relative pronoun ☐

1 mark

32 Read the sentences below. Circle the correct word in brackets to complete each sentence using **Standard English**.

What do you think of **(them / those)** new curtains?

We **(was / were)** just talking about that.

I heard that they put them up really **(quick / quickly)**.

1 mark

33 Read the sentence below.
Tick the word that is an **adverb**.

I don't know what the weather will be like; perhaps it will rain.

Tick **one** box.

know	☐
weather	☐
perhaps	☐
will	☐

1 mark

34 Explain how the different **prefixes** in the two sentences below change their meanings.

The milk bottle was unused.

This means that the bottle _____

_____

The milk bottle was reused.

This means that the bottle _____

_____

1 mark

35 a) Add a **comma** in the sentence below so that it is clear that **only** Hassan and Sarah bought some flowers.

Before they visited Jenny Hassan and Sarah bought some flowers.

1 mark

b) Add **commas** in the sentence below so that it is clear that **all** three children bought some flowers.

Before they visited Jenny Hassan and Sarah bought some flowers.

1 mark

36 Read the sentence below.
Which **word class** does the word '**his**' belong to?

Loreen thanked Pete for **his** present.

Tick **one** box.

verb ☐

adjective ☐

determiner ☐

preposition ☐

1 mark

37 Look at the **word family** below.
What does the root '**cent**' mean in this word family?

century   percent   centipede

Tick **one** box.

creature ☐

one thousand ☐

years ☐

one hundred ☐

1 mark

38 Read the sentences below.
Tick the sentence which uses a **colon** correctly.

Tick **one** box.

Neil doesn't like: swimming he hates getting his hair wet. ☐

Neil doesn't like swimming he hates: getting his hair wet. ☐

Neil doesn't like swimming he: hates getting his hair wet. ☐

Neil doesn't like swimming: he hates getting his hair wet. ☐

1 mark

39 Read the sentence below.
Underline the longest **noun phrase** there is in the sentence.

Alistair went to speak to the quiet young man in the corner.

1 mark

40 The sentence below is missing a **punctuation mark** in the place the arrow is pointing at. Which punctuation mark should be used?

"Your behaviour is unacceptable!" shouted Mrs Bates who was fed up of Toby's rudeness.
↑

Tick **one** box.

exclamation mark ☐

full stop ☐

comma ☐

semi-colon ☐

1 mark

41 Rewrite the sentence below by adding a **subordinate clause** to it. Make sure you use correct punctuation.

Eddie climbed through the window.

_____

_____

1 mark

42 Read the sentence below.
What is '**the high-flying trapeze artist**' an example of?

We went to the circus to see **the high-flying trapeze artist**.

Tick **one** box.

a relative clause ☐

a subordinate clause ☐

a noun phrase ☐

an adverbial phrase ☐

1 mark

43 Read the sentence below.
Insert the missing **semi-colon** so that the sentence is punctuated correctly.

Joan slowly opened the cracked wooden cupboard above the oven it was completely bare.

1 mark

44 The word 'until' can be either a **subordinating conjunction** or a **preposition**. Put a tick in each row to show which form 'until' takes in each sentence.

Sentence	Preposition	Subordinating conjunction
He will work for them **until** next year.		
I had never seen a wolf **until** now.		
Until he apologises, Stephen will not be allowed to play outside.		

1 mark

45 Read the information in the box below. Write one sentence that lists all this information. Make sure you use correct punctuation.

Jake's PE kit
white T-shirt
black shorts
socks
red trainers

_____

_____

1 mark

46 Complete the sentence below by filling in the gaps with the **past progressive** form of the verbs in the boxes.

to do ↓

When I arrived last night, Martha _____ her homework,

to make ↓

and her brothers _____ dinner.

1 mark

47 Read the sentences below.
Tick the sentence which uses the **subjunctive form**.

Tick **one** box.

When I am older, I will be able to drive a car. ☐

If I were older, I would be able to drive a car. ☐

I can't wait to be old enough to drive a car. ☐

In order to drive a car, I must be older. ☐

1 mark

48 Put a letter in each box to show which **word class** the words belong to.

Pete didn't have much milk. He needed to go to the shop soon.

1 mark

49 Read the two sentences below. Explain how the meaning of the sentence is changed when the **commas** are added.

Ricardo thinks Abdul is very clever.

Ricardo, thinks Abdul, is very clever.

_____

_____

1 mark

END OF TEST

[Blank Page]

Key Stage Two English

Set B
Grammar, Punctuation and Spelling

Paper 1: Questions
45 minutes

First name	
Middle name	
Last name	
School	
Date of birth	Day ☐ Month ☐ Year ☐

Paper 2, the spelling task, is a pull-out section in the middle of the booklet.

Total marks ☐

Instructions

This booklet tests your **grammar**, **vocabulary** and **punctuation**. The test has different question types, which you will need to answer in different ways. Each question has a space for you to give your answer. This will show you the type of answer to give:

Multiple-choice answers: you can answer these questions without writing any words. You might have to tick a box, circle a word or draw lines between different words. Read the instructions for each question carefully, as they will tell you what to do.

Short answers: these questions have a line or a box for your answer. This shows that you need to write something. It could be a word, a short phrase or a sentence.

There is a mark box next to each question. It tells you the maximum number of marks for that question.

Do not start until your teacher tells you to. Once you have started the test, work through the booklet until you are told to stop.

You will have 45 minutes to answer all the questions.

1 Read the sentences below.
Tick the sentence which should end with a **question mark**.

Tick **one** box.

I don't know where Alice might be ☐

Where can I meet you after lunch ☐

Where we will be depends on the time ☐

Ask Tyrone where he put the books ☐

1 mark

2 Read the sentences below.
Choose a **conjunction** from the box to fill each gap and write it on the line.
You can only use each conjunction **once**.

| because | if | when |

Mum said that _____ we get home, _____ we get all

of our chores done quickly, we can order a pizza. We can even have

ice cream _____ we've been so helpful lately.

1 mark

3 Tick the most appropriate punctuation mark to end this sentence.

How cold that water is

Tick **one** box.

. ☐

? ☐

! ☐

... ☐

1 mark

4 Read the sentences below.
Circle all of the **adjectives**.

Julia is kind, amazingly clever and incredibly friendly.
She's my best friend.

1 mark

5 Read the sentence below.
Tick the **pair of verbs** which completes the sentence correctly.

Last year, Jayne _____ four pet mice, but now she

_____ six of them.

Tick **one** box.

had	had	☐
had	has	☐
has	had	☐
has	has	☐

1 mark

6 Read the sentence below. Insert the missing **question mark** so that the sentence is punctuated correctly.

" Stephan is outside, isn't he " asked the teacher.

1 mark

7 Read the options below.
Tick the option that uses **full stops** correctly.

Tick **one** box.

I like the zoo. It's more expensive at weekends because that's when they have shows. ☐

I like the zoo. It's more expensive. At weekends because that's when they have shows. ☐

I like the zoo it's more expensive at weekends because that's when they have shows. ☐

I like the zoo it's more expensive at weekends. Because that's when they have shows. ☐

1 mark

8 Read the sentences below.
Circle all of the **pronouns**.

Sophie became a vet because she loves animals.

The training was long — it took her five years to complete.

1 mark

9 Read the sentences below.
Tick the **two** sentences which are **statements**.

Tick **two** boxes.

After dinner, go to the town hall. ☐

I think that there is a meeting taking place. ☐

You must try to see what is happening. ☐

Climb up the ladder to get a better view. ☐

1 mark

10 Read the sentences below.
Tick the sentence which is in the **past tense**.

Tick **one** box.

The slender brown dog is from the shelter. ☐

At the end of my road, a play area is being built. ☐

I have been a mechanic for five years. ☐

The documents were at the back of the drawer. ☐

1 mark

11 Look at the table below. Change the question into a **command**.
Write the command in the right-hand column.

Question	Command
Could you pass the butter?	

1 mark

12 Read the sentences below.
Circle the word that includes an **apostrophe** for **possession**.

Once it's two o'clock, we'll take the cake out of the oven.

There'll be just enough time to decorate it before Samee's party.

1 mark

13 Read the sentences below.
Circle the correct word in brackets to complete each sentence.

I **(did / done)** all of my homework last night.

She ate the sweets **(what / that)** were in the glass jar.

I didn't do **(anything / nothing)** over the weekend.

1 mark

14 Read the sentence below.
Insert **three commas** so that the sentence is punctuated correctly.

Yasmin my best friend has pet mice guinea pigs and fish.

1 mark

15 Underline the **subject** in each of these sentences.

During the storm, Fatima sheltered under a tree.

The key is on the table under those papers.

After some time, the mayor agreed to reopen the park.

1 mark

16 Read the sentence below.
Circle the two words that show the **tense** in the sentence.

On Sunday afternoon, I went to the track and threw javelins.

1 mark

17 Draw lines to match each word to the correct **prefix** to change its meaning.

Prefix   **Word**

un   understand

mis   appear

dis   concerned

1 mark

18 Read the sentences below.
Circle all of the **conjunctions**.

I will come if you promise to keep the dog away from me.

Although the weather was dreadful, we still went for a jog.

Hector and Molly were there, but Duncan couldn't make it.

1 mark

19 Read the sentence below. Replace the underlined word with a **more formal** word. Write the word in the box.

Brian felt <u>lucky</u> to have a close family.

[   ]

1 mark

20 Read the sentences below.
Tick **all** the sentences that contain a **preposition**.

I planted roses opposite my front door. ☐

The postman left the parcel behind the dustbin. ☐

After Solomon had left, there was a loud bang. ☐

I found the cat hiding under the table. ☐

1 mark

21 Insert the missing **inverted commas** into the sentence below.

"Who is it?" asked Erin, as she went to open the door.

1 mark

22 Write your own sentence using the word '**plant**' as a **verb**.
Use the correct punctuation in your sentence. Do not change the word '**plant**'.

_____

1 mark

Write your own sentence using the word '**plant**' as a **noun**.
Use the correct punctuation in your sentence. Do not change the word '**plant**'.

_____

1 mark

Key Stage Two English

Set B
Grammar, Punctuation and Spelling

Paper 2: Spelling

First name	
Middle name	
Last name	
School	

| Date of birth | Day | | Month | | Year | |

Total marks

Spelling Test

1. I was so shocked that I was _____ to speak.

2. Maya is very _____ of Sami's birthday present.

3. The man wanted the hairdresser's _____ .

4. We cut the pizza into _____ .

5. In the _____ , she wants to travel to the moon.

6. The doctor looked for a _____ to give Martha her injection.

7. The children loved _____ new toys.

8. If you shout in a cave, the sound will _____ .

9. His mother told him to keep out of _____ .

10. Even _____ he was tired, he kept going.

11. Jim found the word in the class _____ .

12. Dad asked me to give the car a _____ clean.

13. Mum likes to _____ as she mows the lawn.

14. Bring a Pet to School Day always causes _____ .

15. They will spend the day at the _____ centre.

16. Lena _____ the boxes from the car to the shed.

17. There was a big _____ when the team won.

18. I wrote my _____ on all of my books.

19. She fell off the swing and has a _____ on her leg.

20. Seagulls are _____ if they want your chips.

END OF TEST

[Blank Page]

23 Read the sentences below and circle all the **determiners**.

I feed the cat every night before I go to bed. Then I make sure that there is water in her bowl.

1 mark

24 The sentence below is missing a **dash**.
Tick **one** box to show where the dash should go.

It was difficult to stop the thief she was running away too quickly.

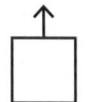 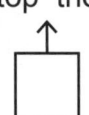 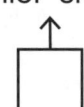 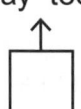

1 mark

25 The sentence below contains **one** error.
Circle the error and write the correction in the box.

The girls was convinced that they had heard a bird in the attic.

[ ]

1 mark

26 Rewrite the sentence below so it starts with the **adverbial**. Only use the words from the sentence, and make sure you use correct punctuation.

Treena is performing in a show in a week's time.

_____

_____

1 mark

27 a) Give an explanation of the word **synonym**.

_____

_____ 1 mark

b) Give one word that is a **synonym** of tired.

_____ 1 mark

28 Read the sentence below and circle the two **adverbs**.

Belle never remembers her homework, although her teacher reminds her regularly.

1 mark

29 Read the sentences below.
Draw a line to show which noun the **pronoun** '**Both**' replaces.

The hikers climbed two mountain peaks in a day. **Both** were exhausted by the time they met some friends in one of the nearby villages that evening.

Pronoun   **Noun**

                      the peaks

                      the hikers

Both

                      the friends

                      the villages

1 mark

30 Read the sentences below.
Tick the **two** sentences which contain a **modal verb**.

Tick **two** boxes.

You should help out in your community. ☐

She played on the swings and the slide. ☐

She can sing really well. ☐

Will likes to hike and ride his bike up mountains. ☐

1 mark

31 Read the sentence below.
Insert the missing **comma** so that the sentence is punctuated correctly.

Near the edge of the park, an old man lives in a small cottage.

1 mark

32 Rewrite the sentence below so that it is in the **passive voice**.
Use the words from the sentence, and add extra words where appropriate.

Taylor fixed my broken computer.

My broken computer was fixed by Taylor.

1 mark

33 Read the sentence below.
Which **word class** does the word '**that**' belong to?

The skirt **that** I saw was green.

Tick **one** box.

noun ☐

relative pronoun ☐

preposition ☐

adverb ☐

1 mark

34 Put a tick in each row of the table to show whether each sentence is in the **present progressive** or the **past progressive**.

Sentence	Present progressive	Past progressive
Grandpa was working hard in his shed all morning.		
Grandpa's tools are lying on the table.		
Grandpa is planning to build a model aeroplane for my sister.		

1 mark

35 Read the passage below. Underline the verb form that is in the **present perfect**.

Derek is my next door neighbour. He moved in over ten years ago.

He has been ill recently so I often mow his lawn for him.

1 mark

36 What is the **name** of the punctuation mark immediately after the word seats in the sentence below?

The people who arrived early got seats; those who arrived late had to stand.

_____

1 mark

37 Read the sentence below.
Tick **one** box which describes the phrase '**who lived up the road**'.

Akshay sent a card to the girl **who lived up the road**.

Tick **one** box.

a main clause ☐

a fronted adverbial ☐

a relative clause ☐

a noun phrase ☐

1 mark

38 Read the sentences below.
Tick the sentence which uses the **hyphen** correctly.

Tick **one** box.

Jess had a part time-job at the supermarket. ☐

Jess had a-part-time-job at the supermarket. ☐

Jess had a part-time job at the supermarket. ☐

Jess had a part-time-job at the supermarket. ☐

1 mark

39 Put a tick in each row of the table below to show whether the conjunction in bold is a **co-ordinating conjunction** or **subordinating conjunction**.

Sentence	Co-ordinating conjunction	Subordinating conjunction
Andy doesn't like heights, **but** he loves going on aeroplanes.		
Get me a burger **while** you're there.		
As I was crossing the road, a deer ran past me.		

1 mark

40 Look at the word in bold below.
Circle all the words which are in the same **word family**.

apply

applause   applied   reapply   disappear   applicant

1 mark

41 Complete the sentence below by filling in the gap with a **possessive pronoun**.

The blue and white car is _____.

1 mark

42 Look at the table below. Add a **suffix** to each noun to make it an adjective.

Noun	Adjective
fun	
poison	
history	
athlete	
colour	

1 mark

43 Read the sentence below. Explain why a **pair of dashes** has been used in this sentence.

The football scarf — bought by Jamie for ten pounds — had mysteriously gone missing.

_____

_____

1 mark

44 Read the sentences below.
Tick the sentence which uses the **subjunctive form**.

Tick **one** box.

I went to Brazil, and I visited the rainforest. ☐

I'll go to Brazil, and I'll visit the rainforest. ☐

If I were to go to Brazil, I would visit the rainforest. ☐

I often go to Brazil and visit the rainforest. ☐

1 mark

45 Look at the table below. Add your own words before and after the noun to make your own **noun phrase**.

One has already been done for you.

Noun	Noun phrase
the shed	the new shed in the garden
the bicycle	

1 mark

46 Complete the sentence below by ticking the option that correctly introduces the **subordinate clause**.

_____ Harvey had spent a lot of money on comics, he still had enough for a new football.

Tick **one** box.

Despite ☐

Even though ☐

Rather than ☐

However ☐

1 mark

47 Read the sentences below.
Tick the sentence which uses **commas** correctly.

Tick **one** box.

My cousins, Ana, and Karl, who I know very well, live in Bath. ☐

My cousins, Ana and Karl who I know very well, live in Bath. ☐

My cousins Ana and Karl, who I know, very well, live in Bath. ☐

My cousins, Ana and Karl, who I know very well, live in Bath. ☐

1 mark

48 Put a tick in each row of the table to show whether the words in **bold** are a **noun phrase** or a **subordinate clause**.

Sentence	Noun phrase	Subordinate clause
I can't walk to school **because it's across town**.		
Our family doctor loves going fishing at the weekends.		
After watching a show about them, Ajay was amazed by sharks.		

1 mark

END OF TEST

[Blank Page]

CGP

Key Stage Two
English
SATS Practice Papers

Instructions with Answers & Mark Scheme

Exam Set EHEP27

Contents

Test Contents 3

Marking the Tests 3

Reading Test Answers.. 4

Grammar, Punctuation and Spelling Paper 1 Answers 12

Grammar, Punctuation and Spelling Paper 2 Scripts/Answers.... 20

Published by CGP

Editors:
Izzy Bowen, Emma Cleasby, Heather Gregson,
Holly Poynton, Frances Rooney, Rebecca Tate, Matt Topping.

With thanks to Emma Bonney and Rebecca Tate for the proofreading.
Also thanks to Jan Greenway for the copyright research.

Clipart from Corel®
Printed by Elanders Ltd, Newcastle upon Tyne.

Text, design and original illustrations
© Coordination Group Publications Ltd. (CGP) 2020
All rights reserved.

Acknowledgements for Answer Booklet:
National Curriculum references on pages 4, 8, 12, 16, 20 and 21 reproduced under the terms of the Open Government Licence v3.0. http://www.nationalarchives.gov.uk/doc/open-government-licence/version/3/

Acknowledgements for Reading Set A:
With thanks to iStock.com for permission to use the images on pages 5, 6, 7 and 8.
With thanks to Katherine Craig for permission to use the image on page 7.
With thanks to Mary Evans for permission to use the images on pages 9 and 11.

Acknowledgements for Reading Set B:
With thanks to iStock.com for permission to use the image on page 7.
Image on pg 11 © Bilby licenced for re-use under the Creative Commons Attribution 3.0 Unported Licence.
https://creativecommons.org/licenses/by/3.0/deed.en

Photocopying more than 5% of a paper is not permitted, even if you have a CLA licence.
Extra copies are available from CGP with next day delivery • 0800 1712 712 • www.cgpbooks.co.uk

Test Contents

There are **two sets** of practice papers in this pack.
Each set has:

Reading Test   **50 marks**
1 hour
(reading booklet, and question and answer booklet)

Grammar, Punctuation and Spelling Paper 1 — Questions   **50 marks**
45 minutes
(question and answer booklet)

Grammar, Punctuation and Spelling Paper 2 — Spelling Task   **20 marks**
About 15 minutes
(pull-out question and answer booklet found in the middle of Grammar, Punctuation and Spelling Paper 1)

*The Spelling Task needs to be read out to the child sitting the test.
The Spelling Task Scripts can be found on pages 22 and 23 of this booklet.*

Marking the Tests

The scores for these practice papers will give you a pretty good idea of whether a pupil is on track to achieve the **expected standard** in **Reading** and in **Grammar, Punctuation and Spelling**.

Reading

There's a total of **50** marks available.

The mark needed to achieve the **expected standard** varies from year to year, but if they get a total of **21** or more then they should be on track.

Grammar, Punctuation and Spelling

	Marks available
Paper 1: Short Answer Questions	50
Paper 2: Spelling Task	20
Total:	70

Add up the marks in the two papers to give a score out of **70**. Again, the mark needed to achieve the **expected standard** varies from year to year, but if they get a total of **44** or more then they should be on track. (The writing element of the national curriculum is assessed by the class teacher.)

KS2 English — Answers & Mark Scheme

Set A: Reading

Content Domain Coverage

(Shows the aspects of reading assessed in the Set A reading paper)

	2a	2b	2c	2d	2e	2f	2g	2h
	Give / explain the meaning of words in context.	Retrieve and record information / identify key details from fiction and non-fiction.	Summarise main ideas from more than one paragraph.	Make inferences from the text / explain and justify inferences with evidence from the text.	Predict what might happen from details stated and implied.	Identify / explain how information / narrative content is related and contributes to meaning as a whole.	Identify / explain how meaning is enhanced through choice of words and phrases.	Make comparisons within the text.
Qu.				**Section 1 – Keeping Fit**				
1		1						
2								1
3	1							
4		1						
5			1					
6		1						
7a		1						
7b		1						
7c		1						
8			1					
9		1						
10					2			
11						1		
Qu.				**Section 2 – A Day of Surprises**				
12				1				
13		1						
14				1				
15	1							
16	1							
17	1							
18				1				
19				1				
20		1						
21				1				
22				2				
23	2							
24						1		
25				3				
Qu.				**Section 3 – Harry Houdini**				
26		1						
27		1						
28	1							
29			1					
30	1							
31							2	
32				1				
33		1						
34	1							
35		1						
36				1				
37				1				
38			2					
39				3				

KS2 English — Answers & Mark Scheme © CGP 2020

Set A: Reading – Answers

Section 1 — Keeping Fit

Qu.	Answer	Marking notes	Marks (Domain)
1	An hour		1 (2b)
2	Refers to children needing more exercise than the amount recommended for adults under 65.		1 (2h)
3	demands		1 (2a)
4	It prepares your body for exercise. It increases the blood flow to muscles, providing them with oxygen. It increases sweat production to maintain correct body temperature. It reduces the risk of damaging your muscles during exercise.	1 mark for reference to any of the acceptable answers.	1 (2b)
5	How to warm up correctly		1 (2c)
6	Doing exercise can make you feel happier. — True Adults under 65 should do strength-building activities for two-and-a-half hours a week. — False Warming up makes you sweat more. — True You should move your feet around when you're doing body twists. — False	1 mark for all 4 correct.	1 (2b)
7a	aerobic exercises.		1 (2b)
7b	rock climbing.		1 (2b)
7c	reduce injuries.		1 (2b)
8	Refers to the idea that different types of exercise involve doing different activities. Refers to the importance of doing different types of exercise. Refers to the idea that different types of exercise have different effects / benefits. **Do not accept** answers that mention a specific fact, rather than an overall idea.	1 mark for reference to any of the acceptable answers.	1 (2c)
9	walking slowly doing stretches	1 mark for reference to either.	1 (2b)
10	Acceptable points and possible evidence: • They might injure themselves, e.g. because warming up reduces the risk of 'muscle damage'. • They might get dizzy, e.g. because cooling down helps to 'prevent drops in blood pressure'. • They might get sore or sick, e.g. because cooling down helps to 'remove any lactic acid'. • They might get too hot or too cold, e.g. because a good warm-up will increase 'sweat production' to maintain ideal body temperature. • They might not be ready for exercise, e.g. because warming up is 'crucial' before exercising.	1 mark for 1 acceptable point. 2 marks for 2 acceptable points, or 1 acceptable point supported with evidence.	2 (2e)
11	Refers to the text following the order that you should exercise in. **Do not accept** answers that reference the text being a guide on how to exercise.		1 (2f)

Section 2 — A Day of Surprises

Qu.	Answer	Marking notes	Marks (Domain)
12	Refers to Emily being awake before her alarm clock sounded. Refers to Emily leaping out of bed / flinging back her duvet. Refers to Emily being ready a long time before her dad was up.	1 mark for reference to any of the acceptable answers.	1 (2d)
13	Saturday		1 (2b)
14	Refers to Auntie Jane being mysterious / secretive. Refers to Auntie Jane being fun / exciting. Refers to Auntie Jane being fashionable / cultured.	1 mark for reference to any of the acceptable answers.	1 (2d)
15	Refers to Emily and Jane sitting comfortably. Refers to Emily and Jane fitting snugly into their seats.	1 mark for reference to either of the acceptable answers.	1 (2a)
16	It's busy.		1 (2a)
17	Refers to the stories being gruesome / horrible / unpleasant. Refers to the stories being horror stories / being scary.	1 mark for reference to either of the acceptable answers.	1 (2a)
18	disappointed but grateful		1 (2d)
19	Refers to Emily being disappointed that they had not seen Rosie Ambrose. Refers to Auntie Jane knowing Emily was upset. **Do not accept** answers that simply mention Emily not eating her pasta.	1 mark for reference to either of the acceptable answers.	1 (2d)
20	walking and train	1 mark for both answers correct.	1 (2b)
21	Refers to the sky getting darker. Refers to the buses turning their headlights on.	1 mark for reference to either of the acceptable answers.	1 (2d)
22	Acceptable points: • Rosie Ambrose is mentioned a lot in the text. • Emily has an image of Rosie printed on her duvet. • Emily gets up early because she thinks she's going to meet Rosie. • Emily is described as 'restless' because she thinks she's going to meet Rosie. • Emily 'beamed' at the poster of Rosie. • Emily had 'craved' Rosie's signature for years. • Emily is disappointed / upset when she thinks she isn't meeting Rosie. • Her heart is 'racing uncontrollably' when she thinks she's going to meet Rosie. • Her face is a 'picture of delight' when she hears Rosie's song.	1 mark for 1 acceptable point. 2 marks for 2 acceptable points.	2 (2d)
23	Recognition that it means an autograph in the first context. Recognition that it means a special, unique item or an item that is famously owned by someone in the second context.	1 mark for each correct definition.	2 (2a)
24	Emily hums one of Rosie Ambrose's songs. — 3 Emily meets one of Auntie Jane's friends. — 5 Emily admires a poster of Rosie Ambrose. — 2 Auntie Jane and Emily stop to have lunch. — 4 Auntie Jane promises Emily a birthday surprise. — 1	1 mark for all 4 correct.	1 (2f)
25	Acceptable points and possible evidence: • Disappointed, e.g. her expression was 'like a grimace' when she thought the Tower of London was the main surprise. • Grumpy, e.g. Emily 'dragged herself around the tower'. • Preoccupied, e.g. 'her mind was preoccupied' that she'd missed the chance to meet Rosie. • Confused, e.g. Emily was left confused when Auntie Jane would 'say no more'. • Intrigued, e.g. Emily wondered what the real surprise Jane had planned was. • Excited, e.g. her heart was 'racing' before meeting Rosie. • Happy, e.g. Emily's face was a 'picture of delight' when she met Rosie.	1 mark for 1 acceptable point. 2 marks for 2 acceptable points, or 1 acceptable point supported with evidence. 3 marks for 2 acceptable points, with at least one supported with evidence.	3 (2d)

Section 3 — Harry Houdini

Qu.	Answer	Marking notes	Marks (Domain)
26	1878		1 (2b)
27	Refers to having read a book about Robert Houdin.		1 (2b)
28	toiling		1 (2a)
29	Complete sentence that references the idea that his life was difficult before he became an escape artist. **Do not accept** answers that summarise his life after he became an escape artist.	1 mark for a complete sentence that references the acceptable answer.	1 (2c)
30	Daring acts		1 (2a)
31	danger imprisoned hurled sea monster trapped survived dangling perilously buried alive	1 mark for 1 or 2 words/phrases, 2 marks for 3 words/phrases.	2 (2g)
32	Recognition that the reader may be fearful / scared. Recognition that the reader may feel admiration for Houdini.	1 mark for reference to either.	1 (2d)
33	magic planes cinema	1 mark for reference to any of the acceptable answers.	1 (2b)
34	speculation		1 (2a)
35	Refers to the fact that he tried to disprove the psychic's claims. **Do not accept** answers that simply state he disagreed with psychics.		1 (2b)
36	Houdini died because he was hit in the stomach. — Opinion Harry was a good actor. — Opinion There was a stamp which featured Harry Houdini. — Fact Houdini wanted to help the war effort. — Fact	1 mark for all 4 correct.	1 (2d)
37	Refers to the fact that people liked / admired / respected Houdini. Refers to the fact that people felt sad at his death.	1 mark for reference to either.	1 (2d)
38	Acceptable points: • He created his own magic act at a young age. • He 'toiled away' at his magic even though he didn't have success. • He did magic and escape artistry from his early life until he died. • He had 'many other interests' but he never stopped doing escape artistry. • He wanted the challenge of more difficult tasks. • He risked his life to perform his tricks.	1 mark for 1 acceptable point. 2 marks for 2 acceptable points.	2 (2c)
39	Acceptable points and possible evidence: • Helpful, e.g. taught the soldiers how to escape bonds. • Hard-working, e.g. had a 'variety of jobs' to support his family. • Brave, e.g. did frightening acts such as being 'buried alive'. • Determined, e.g. worked hard despite only having 'modest success' initially. • Clever, e.g. able to attract publicity by performing in police stations. • Reckless, e.g. may have died because he claimed he could 'take any blow'.	1 mark for 1 acceptable point. 2 marks for 2 acceptable points, or 1 acceptable point supported with evidence. 3 marks for 3 acceptable points, or 2 acceptable points, with at least 1 supported with evidence.	3 (2d)

Set B: Reading

Content Domain Coverage

(Shows the aspects of reading assessed in the Set B reading paper)

	2a	2b	2c	2d	2e	2f	2g	2h
	Give / explain the meaning of words in context.	Retrieve and record information / identify key details from fiction and non-fiction.	Summarise main ideas from more than one paragraph.	Make inferences from the text / explain and justify inferences with evidence from the text.	Predict what might happen from details stated and implied.	Identify / explain how information / narrative content is related and contributes to meaning as a whole.	Identify / explain how meaning is enhanced through choice of words and phrases.	Make comparisons within the text.
Qu.				Section 1 – The Wonderful Wizard of Oz				
1		1						
2	1							
3				1				
4				1				
5							1	
6		1						
7	1							
8				1				
9						1		
10					2			
11				2				
12			3					
Qu.				Section 2 – Earthquakes				
13		1						
14				1				
15		1						
16								1
17	1							
18		1						
19		2						
20				1				
21			1					
22			2					
23				1				
24				1				
25				3				
Qu.				Section 3 – Talking Through Time				
26	2							
27				1				
28a		1						
28b		1						
28c		1						
28d		1						
29		1						
30		1						
31				1				
32	1							
33				1				
34								2
35	1							
36						1		
37				1				

Set B: Reading – Answers

Section 1 — The Wonderful Wizard of Oz

Qu.	Answer	Marking notes	Marks (Domain)
1	in a cottage		1 (2b)
2	troublesome		1 (2a)
3	Recognition that the reader could feel scared / nervous. Recognition that the reader could feel concerned for the characters' safety.	1 mark for reference to either.	1 (2d)
4	Refers to Toto being scared / surprised. Refers to Toto wanting to protect Dorothy and the Scarecrow. Refers to Toto being fearless. Refers to Toto being aggressive.	1 mark for reference to any of the acceptable answers.	1 (2d)
5	moved by **Do not accept** answers that only reference the Tin Woodman's 'sad voice'.		1 (2g)
6	Refers to the Tin Woodman saying 'my cottage'. Refers to Dorothy saying 'your cottage'. Recognition that the Tin Woodman's oil can is in the cottage.	1 mark for reference to any of the acceptable answers.	1 (2b)
7	happiness		1 (2a)
8	Refers to the Tin Woodman saying she saved his life. Refers to the Tin Woodman saying he might have stood there forever / wouldn't be able to move were it not for Dorothy. Refers to the Tin Woodman being 'very grateful' / thanking them 'again and again'.	1 mark for reference to any of the acceptable answers.	1 (2d)
9	Dorothy oils the Tin Woodman's legs. — 4 Dorothy wakes up. — 1 Dorothy explains why she wants to see the Wizard. — 5 Toto bites the Tin Woodman. — 3 Dorothy washes in the spring. — 2	1 mark for all 4 correct.	1 (2f)
10	Acceptable points (yes): • Dorothy has already let the scarecrow join her on her journey. • Dorothy helped him, showing she cares about him. • He is a 'very polite creature' so they will like him. • They believe the Wizard of Oz will be able to give him a heart. **Do not accept** answers that speculate about allowing the Tin Woodman to join them without reference to what has happened in the text to motivate them.	1 mark for 1 acceptable point. 2 marks for 2 acceptable points.	2 (2e)
11	Acceptable points (yes): • Dorothy investigates the noise, even though it made her nervous. • Dorothy helps the Tin Woodman despite being 'stopped short' and surprised by him. Acceptable points (no): • Dorothy asks about the noise 'timidly', suggesting she is scared. • She gives a 'little cry of surprise' upon seeing the Tin Woodman, which might also show she is scared.	1 mark for 1 acceptable point. 2 marks for 2 acceptable points.	2 (2d)
12	Acceptable points and possible evidence: • Oz is referred to as magical, e.g. in the introduction it's called a 'magical land'. • A scarecrow is alive / can speak, e.g. he talks to Dorothy. • A figure made of tin is alive / can speak, e.g. he 'gave a sigh'. • Both characters defy reality, e.g. they exist without 'a brain' / 'a heart'. • There is a wizard, e.g. Dorothy mentions the 'Great Oz'. • The wizard is thought to be magic, e.g. they want him to give the Scarecrow brains.	1 mark for 1 acceptable point. 2 marks for 2 acceptable points, or 1 acceptable point supported with evidence. 3 marks for 3 acceptable points, or 2 acceptable points, with at least 1 supported with evidence.	3 (2c)

Section 2 — Earthquakes

Qu.	Answer	Marking notes	Marks (Domain)
13	Recognition that it is a way to measure the severity of earthquakes.		1 (2b)
14	Recognition that a jigsaw is an image readers will be familiar with, so the comparison allows them to picture the Earth's plates more clearly.		1 (2d)
15	Japan — **2011** **USA** — 1999 New Zealand — **2011**	1 mark for all 3 correct.	1 (2b)
16	Refers to there being fewer people / buildings in the Mojave Desert. Refers to there being more people / buildings in Christchurch.	1 mark for reference to either of the acceptable answers.	1 (2h)
17	essential		1 (2a)
18	Recognition that indicators of an earthquake don't always appear before an earthquake.		1 (2b)
19	strapping down heavy pieces of furniture using putty to secure smaller objects fixing taller pieces of furniture to walls fitting flexible pipes	1 mark for 2 correct answers. 2 marks for 3 correct answers.	2 (2b)
20	Refers to helping the people of Japan to be prepared / remain safe during earthquakes. **Do not accept** simple reference to Japan being in an earthquake zone.		1 (2d)
21	Earthquake preparations		1 (2c)
22	Acceptable points (during): • Drop to the floor. • Shield your head. • Take cover under a table. Acceptable points (after): • Stay in the same place until any aftershocks subside. • Look after others. • Check for any damage to buildings / houses. • Evacuate people if buildings / houses are badly damaged.	1 mark for any 1 acceptable point referring to during an earthquake. 1 mark for any 1 acceptable point referring to after an earthquake.	2 (2c)
23	Recognition that a torch wouldn't ignite gas leaks, but a candle / match would.		1 (2d)
24	Recognition that dust is bad for you and that a dust mask will prevent / reduce dust inhalation.		1 (2d)
25	Acceptable points (yes): • Most earthquakes are small / unnoticeable, so people don't always get hurt. • Scientists can sometimes predict when an earthquake will occur, so people can prepare themselves. • Refers to any of the various ways of preparing / designing buildings for an earthquake, so people aren't hurt. Acceptable points (no): • Not all earthquakes can be predicted, meaning people can't always fully prepare for them. • People are hurt in earthquakes even when countries are prepared. • Buildings are damaged in earthquakes even when countries are prepared. **Do not accept** answers that do not reference evidence from the text.	1 mark for 1 acceptable point. 2 marks for 2 acceptable points. 3 marks for 3 acceptable points.	3 (2d)

Section 3 — Talking Through Time

Qu.	Answer	Marking notes	Marks (Domain)
26	instantly — started transporting — sending (crossed) originated — service (crossed) facility — rapidly	1 mark for 2 correct answers. 2 marks for all 4 answers correct.	2 (2a)
27	The King		1 (2d)
28a	how far it travelled.		1 (2b)
28b	individuals on horses.		1 (2b)
28c	1840.		1 (2b)
28d	postcodes.		1 (2b)
29	Refers to the idea that lots of people were working on similar inventions at the same time.		1 (2b)
30	In America, the first telephone line was completed in 1877. — True By 1878, there were almost 48,000 telephones in America. — False Early telephones were connected together in pairs by a long wire. — True A switchboard to swap the wires was invented in 1895. — False	1 mark for all 4 correct.	1 (2b)
31	Refers to PCs becoming smaller / less unwieldy. Refers to PCs becoming cheaper. **Do not accept** the idea that people wanted more ways to communicate.	1 mark for reference to either of the acceptable answers.	1 (2d)
32	Refers to the idea that there was a dramatic increase in the amount of people using the internet. Refers to the idea that internet use increased very quickly.	1 mark for reference to either of the acceptable answers.	1 (2a)
33	Recognition that more people using the internet means there are more people to email / more emails are sent.		1 (2d)
34	Refers to smartphones being able to play videos / early telephones couldn't. Refers to smartphones being able to connect to the internet / early telephones couldn't. Refers to smartphones being able to send and receive emails / early telephones couldn't. Refers to smartphones being portable / early telephones were connected by a wire. **Do not accept** simple reference to the idea that smartphones can do more / have more features.	1 mark for 1 acceptable point. 2 marks for 2 acceptable points.	2 (2h)
35	tried / attempted		1 (2a)
36	Refers to the introduction and the box on page 11 both mentioning changes in communication through time. Refers to the difficulty of communicating in the past compared to the relative ease of present-day communication.	1 mark for reference to either of the acceptable answers.	1 (2f)
37	Royal Mail sent the first public overseas airmail in the 1900s. — Fact Telegrams are the best form of communication. — Opinion Mobile phones were first available to the public in 1984. — Fact Personal computers were the most important invention of the 1900s. — Opinion	1 mark for all 4 correct.	1 (2d)

Set A: Grammar, Punctuation and Spelling Paper 1

Content Domain Coverage

The table below shows the aspects of grammar, punctuation and spelling assessed in Set A paper 1.

Qu.	Content domain reference	Mark
1	G5.1: Capital letters	1
2	G5.2: Full stops G5.3: Question marks G5.4: Exclamation marks	1
3	G5.2: Full stops	1
4	G1.1: Nouns	1
5	G1.4: Conjunctions	1
6	G5.8: Apostrophes	1
7	G5.12: Single dashes	1
8	G2.3: Commands	1
9	G2.2: Questions	1
10	G5.4: Exclamation marks	1
11	G5.14: Bullet points	1
12	G1.5: Pronouns	1
13	G2.1: Statements G2.3: Commands	1
14	G6.1: Synonyms and antonyms	1
15	G5.8: Apostrophes	1
16	G2.2: Questions	1
17	G1.6: Adverbs	1
18	G1.4: Conjunctions	1
19	G3.1a: Relative clauses	1
20	G1.2: Verbs G1.9: Subject and object	1
21	G7.3: Formal and informal structures	1
22	G4.1a: Simple past and simple present	1
23	G1.3: Adjectives	1
24	G5.9: Punctuation for parenthesis	1
25	G2: Functions of sentences	1
26	G5.7: Inverted commas	1
27	G4.1c: Modal verbs	1

Qu.	Content domain reference	Mark
28	G4.4: Passive and active	1
29	G5.13: Hyphens	1
30	G1.6: Adverbs	1
31	G1.5b: Relative pronouns	1
32	G7.1: Standard English	1
33	G1.6: Adverbs	1
34	G6.2: Prefixes	1
35a	G5.6a: Commas to clarify meaning	1
35b	G5.5: Commas in lists G5.6a: Commas to clarify meaning	1
36	G1.8: Determiners	1
37	G6.4: Word families	1
38	G5.10: Colons	1
39	G3.2: Noun phrases	1
40	G5.9: Punctuation for parenthesis	1
41	G3.4: Subordinating conjunctions and subordinate clauses	1
42	G3.2: Noun phrases	1
43	G5.11: Semi-colons	1
44	G1.7: Prepositions G3.4: Subordinating conjunctions and subordinate clauses	1
45	G5.5: Commas in lists	1
46	G4.1d: Present and past progressive	1
47	G4.3: Subjunctive verb forms	1
48	G1.1: Nouns G1.5: Pronouns G1.6: Adverbs G1.8: Determiners	1
49	G5.6a: Commas to clarify meaning	1

Set A: Grammar, Punctuation and Spelling Paper 1 – Answers

Qu.	Answer	Marking notes	Marks (Domain)
1	we, egypt, my, karen and i	1 mark for all 5 correct.	1 (G5.1)
2	Where did Farid go — ? William could come for lunch — ! What a brilliant performance that was — .	1 mark for all 3 correct.	1 (G5.2 G5.3 G5.4)
3	I love to read. My favourite books are thrillers.		1 (G5.2)
4	hope		1 (G1.1)

Qu.	Answer	Marking notes	Marks (Domain)
5	You can go to the shop <u>and</u> buy a DVD <u>unless</u> you would rather get a game. You can choose <u>as</u> it's your pocket money.	1 mark for all 3 correct.	1 (G1.4)
6	won't		1 (G5.8)
7	dash		1 (G5.12)
8	Close the door.	1 mark for a grammatically correct sentence which is correctly punctuated.	1 (G2.3)
9	can't you		1 (G2.2)
10	"I don't want to go to the museum↑" cried Seb. ✓		1 (G5.4)
11	From the shop, Colin needs: • bread • butter • ham • cheese	1 mark for all 4 correct. If the answer uses capitalisation, it should do so at the start of each point. If the answer uses punctuation, it should use either commas or semi-colons after the first three points and a full stop after the fourth.	1 (G5.14)
12	his mine		1 (G1.5)
13		Sentence	Statement	Command
---	---	---
You must bring her some more food.	✓	
Jameela asked for some more food.	✓	
Go to the kitchen if you want more food.		✓		1 mark for all 3 correct.	1 (G2.1 G2.3)
14	continuous — intermittent doubt — trust robust — delicate conform — oppose	1 mark for all 4 correct.	1 (G6.1)
15	Shes, Mums and dont	1 mark for all 3 correct.	1 (G5.8)
16	Answers may vary, for example: 	Question	Answer
---	---
What is your favourite colour?	Purple.
What do you think of my new dress?	I love it!
What do you do at the weekend?	I go swimming.		1 mark for 2 grammatically correct sentences which are correctly punctuated using a capital letter and a question mark.	1 (G2.2)
17	Answers may vary, for example: happily quietly	1 mark for an appropriate adverb.	1 (G1.6)
18	If, and and as	1 mark for all 3 correct.	1 (G1.4)

Qu.	Answer	Marking notes	Marks (Domain)
19	Sally forgot that the curry which Jim had made was still in the oven. (tick under "which Jim had made")		1 (G3.1a)
20	Kirsten opened the door. S — V — O	1 mark for all 3 correct.	1 (G1.2 G1.9)
21	Kathryn has requested that we eat beef. The dessert was equally delicious.	1 mark for both correct.	1 (G7.3)
22	grow → grew dislikes → disliked begin → began	1 mark for all 3 correct. Answers must be spelt correctly.	1 (G4.1a)
23	Although horse riding can be dangerous, with good training you can learn to ride safely. In my <u>personal</u> opinion, horses are <u>beautiful</u> animals.	1 mark for both correct.	1 (G1.3)
24	My English teacher (Mrs Ferraz) runs the local book club.		1 (G5.9)
25	What a scary lion we saw at the zoo — exclamation Don't stand too close to the lion enclosure — command What time will the lions be fed at the zoo — question There are six lions and two cubs at this zoo — statement	1 mark for all 4 correct.	1 (G2)
26	Answers may vary, for example: Samantha asked him, "Would you like a new jumper?" Samantha asked him, "Would you like to have a new jumper?"	1 mark for a grammatically correct question which is correctly punctuated using speech marks and a question mark in the appropriate places.	1 (G5.7)
27	I shall go to the cinema tomorrow.		1 (G4.1c)
28	The farmer apologised for the delays.		1 (G4.4)
29	We had lunch at a nice family owned café last weekend. (tick under "family")		1 (G5.13)
30		Adverb	Time	Place
---	---	---
yesterday	✓	
near		✓
rarely	✓	
behind		✓		1 mark for all 4 correct.	1 (G1.6)
31	a relative pronoun		1 (G1.5b)
32	those, were and quickly	1 mark for all 3 correct.	1 (G7.1)
33	perhaps		1 (G1.6)

Qu.	Answer	Marking notes	Marks (Domain)
34	Answers may vary; accept any two suitable explanations, for example: The milk bottle was <u>unused</u>. This means that the bottle had not been used before. The milk bottle was <u>reused</u>. This means that the bottle was being used again.	1 mark for both correct. Do not deduct marks for misspellings.	1 (G6.2)
35a	Before they visited Jenny, Hassan and Sarah bought some flowers.		1 (G5.6a)
35b	Before they visited, Jenny, Hassan and Sarah bought some flowers.		1 (G5.5 G5.6a)
36	determiner		1 (G1.8)
37	one hundred		1 (G6.4)
38	Neil doesn't like swimming: he hates getting his hair wet.		1 (G5.10)
39	Alistair went to speak to <u>the quiet young man in the corner</u>.		1 (G3.2)
40	comma		1 (G5.9)
41	Answers may vary, for example: Eddie climbed through the window <u>when he couldn't find his keys</u>. Eddie climbed through the window <u>after realising the door was locked</u>. <u>Upon seeing the fire,</u> Eddie climbed through the window.	1 mark for any sentence where a subordinate clause has been added correctly.	1 (G3.4)
42	a noun phrase		1 (G3.2)
43	Joan slowly opened the cracked wooden cupboard above the oven; it was completely bare.		1 (G5.11)
44		Sentence	Preposition	Subordinating conjunction
---	---	---
He will work for them **until** next year.	✓	
I had never seen a wolf **until** now.	✓	
Until he apologises, Stephen will not be allowed to play outside.		✓		1 mark for all 3 correct.	1 (G1.7 G3.4)
45	Answers may vary, for example: Jake's PE kit contains a white T-shirt, black shorts, socks and a pair of red trainers. In Jake's PE kit, there was a white T-shirt, black shorts, socks and a pair of red trainers.	1 mark for any suitable sentence which lists all the information and is punctuated correctly.	1 (G5.5)
46	When I arrived last night, Martha <u>was doing</u> her homework, and her brothers <u>were making</u> dinner.	1 mark for both correct. Answers must be spelt correctly.	1 (G4.1d)
47	If I were older, I would be able to drive a car.		1 (G4.3)
48	Pete didn't have much milk. He needed to go to the shop soon. ↑ C ↑ A ↑ B ↑ D	1 mark for all 4 correct.	1 (G1.1 G1.5 G1.6 G1.8)
49	The first sentence suggests Ricardo thinks that Abdul is very clever. The second sentence suggests Abdul thinks that Ricardo is very clever.	Do not deduct marks for misspellings.	1 (G5.6a)

Set B: Grammar, Punctuation and Spelling Paper 1

Content Domain Coverage

The table below shows the aspects of grammar, punctuation and spelling assessed in Set B paper 1.

Qu.	Content domain reference	Mark
1	G5.3: Question marks	1
2	G1.4: Conjunctions	1
3	G5.4: Exclamation marks	1
4	G1.3: Adjectives	1
5	G4.1a: Simple past and simple present	1
6	G5.3: Question marks	1
7	G5.2: Full stops	1
8	G1.5: Pronouns	1
9	G2.1: Statements	1
10	G4.1a: Simple past and simple present	1
11	G2.3: Commands	1
12	G5.8: Apostrophes	1
13	G7.1: Standard English	1
14	G5.5: Commas in lists G5.9: Punctuation for parenthesis	1
15	G1.9: Subject and object	1
16	G4.2: Tense consistency	1
17	G6.2: Prefixes	1
18	G1.4: Conjunctions	1
19	G7.2: Formal and informal vocabulary	1
20	G1.7: Prepositions	1
21	G5.7: Inverted commas	1
22	G1.1: Nouns G1.2: Verbs	2
23	G1.8: Determiners	1
24	G5.12: Single dashes	1
25	G7.1: Standard English	1
26	G1.6a: Adverbials	1

Qu.	Content domain reference	Mark
27a	G6.1: Synonyms and antonyms	1
27b	G6.1: Synonyms and antonyms	1
28	G1.6: Adverbs	1
29	G1.5: Pronouns	1
30	G4.1c: Modal verbs	1
31	G5.6b: Commas after fronted adverbials	1
32	G4.4: Passive and active	1
33	G1.5b: Relative pronouns	1
34	G4.1d: Present and past progressive	1
35	G4.1b: Verbs in the perfect form	1
36	G5.11: Semi-colons	1
37	G3.1a: Relative clauses	1
38	G5.13: Hyphens	1
39	G3.3: Co-ordinating conjunctions G3.4: Subordinating conjunctions and subordinate clauses	1
40	G6.4: Word families	1
41	G1.5a: Possessive pronouns	1
42	G6.3: Suffixes	1
43	G5.9: Punctuation for parenthesis	1
44	G4.3: Subjunctive verb forms	1
45	G3.2: Noun phrases	1
46	G3.4: Subordinating conjunctions and subordinate clauses	1
47	G5.9: Punctuation for parenthesis	1
48	G3.2: Noun phrases G3.4: Subordinating conjunctions and subordinate clauses	1

Set B: Grammar, Punctuation and Spelling Paper 1 – Answers

Qu.	Answer	Marking notes	Marks (Domain)
1	Where can I meet you after lunch		1 (G5.3)
2	Mum said that <u>when</u> we get home, <u>if</u> we get all of our chores done quickly, we can order a pizza. We can even have ice cream <u>because</u> we've been so helpful lately.	1 mark for all 3 correct.	1 (G1.4)
3	!		1 (G5.4)
4	kind, clever, friendly and best	1 mark for all 4 correct.	1 (G1.3)
5	had has		1 (G4.1a)
6	"Stephan is outside, isn't he?" asked the teacher.		1 (G5.3)
7	I like the zoo. It's more expensive at weekends because that's when they have shows.		1 (G5.2)

Qu.	Answer	Marking notes	Marks (Domain)
8	she, it and her	1 mark for all 3 correct.	1 (G1.5)
9	I think that there is a meeting taking place. You must try to see what is happening.	1 mark for both correct.	1 (G2.1)
10	The documents were at the back of the drawer.		1 (G4.1a)
11	Pass the butter.	1 mark for a grammatically correct sentence which is correctly punctuated.	1 (G2.3)
12	Samee's		1 (G5.8)
13	I <u>did</u> all of my homework last night. She ate the sweets <u>that</u> were in the glass jar. I didn't do <u>anything</u> over the weekend.	1 mark for all 3 correct.	1 (G7.1)
14	Yasmin, my best friend, has pet mice, guinea pigs and fish.	1 mark for all 3 correct.	1 (G5.5 G5.9)
15	During the storm, <u>Fatima</u> sheltered under a tree. <u>The key</u> is on the table under those papers. After some time, <u>the mayor</u> agreed to reopen the park.	1 mark for all 3 correct.	1 (G1.9)
16	went and threw	1 mark for both correct.	1 (G4.2)
17	un — concerned, mis — understand, dis — appear	1 mark for all 3 correct.	1 (G6.2)
18	if, Although, and and but	1 mark for all 4 correct.	1 (G1.4)
19	Answers may vary, for example: fortunate blessed	1 mark for any suitable, formal synonym.	1 (G7.2)
20	I planted roses opposite my front door. The postman left the parcel behind the dustbin. I found the cat hiding under the table.	1 mark for all 3 correct.	1 (G1.7)
21	"Who is it?" asked Erin, as she went to open the door.		1 (G5.7)
22	Verb — answers may vary, for example: April is a good time to plant your sunflowers outside. Noun — answers may vary, for example: Alan bought a tall plant at the garden centre.	1 mark per suitable sentence. Sentences must be grammatically correct, punctuated correctly and contain an appropriate verb or noun. **Do not accept** answers in which the given word has been changed.	2 (G1.1 G1.2)
23	the, every and her	1 mark for all 3 correct.	1 (G1.8)
24	It was difficult to stop the thief ↑✓ she was running away too quickly.		1 (G5.12)
25	The error is 'was'. The correct word is 'were'.	1 mark if 'was' is circled and 'were' is written in the box.	1 (G7.1)
26	In a week's time, Treena is performing in a show.		1 (G1.6a)

KS2 English — Answers & Mark Scheme

Qu.	Answer	Marking notes	Marks (Domain)
27a	Answers may vary, for example: A word that means the same or nearly the same as another word.	1 mark for a correct explanation of the word synonym. Do not deduct marks for errors in spelling, punctuation and grammar.	1 (G6.1)
27b	Answers may vary, for example: weary exhausted		1 (G6.1)
28	never and regularly	1 mark for both correct.	1 (G1.6)
29	Both — the hikers		1 (G1.5)
30	You should help out in your community. She can sing really well.	1 mark for both correct.	1 (G4.1c)
31	Near the edge of the park, an old man lives in a small cottage.		1 (G5.6b)
32	Answers may vary, for example: My broken computer was fixed by Taylor. My broken computer has been fixed by Taylor.	1 mark for an answer correctly written in the passive voice that uses all the words from the sentence.	1 (G4.4)
33	relative pronoun		1 (G1.5b)

Question 34:

Sentence	Present progressive	Past progressive
Grandpa was working hard in his shed all morning.		✓
Grandpa's tools are lying on the table.	✓	
Grandpa is planning to build a model aeroplane for my sister.	✓	

1 mark for all 3 correct. — 1 (G4.1d)

Qu.	Answer	Marking notes	Marks
35	has been		1 (G4.1b)
36	semi-colon		1 (G5.11)
37	a relative clause		1 (G3.1a)
38	Jess had a part-time job at the supermarket.		1 (G5.13)

Question 39:

Sentence	Co-ordinating conjunction	Subordinating conjunction
Andy doesn't like heights, **but** he loves going on aeroplanes.	✓	
Get me a burger **while** you're there.		✓
As I was crossing the road, a deer ran past me.		✓

1 mark for all 3 correct. — 1 (G3.3 G3.4)

| 40 | applied, reapply and applicant | 1 mark for all 3 correct. | 1 (G6.4) |

Qu.	Answer	Marking notes	Marks (Domain)
41	Answers may vary, for example: mine hers theirs	1 mark for any possessive pronoun.	1 (G1.5a)
42	<table><tr><th>Noun</th><th>Adjective</th></tr><tr><td>fun</td><td>funny</td></tr><tr><td>poison</td><td>poisonous / poisoned</td></tr><tr><td>history</td><td>historic / historical</td></tr><tr><td>athlete</td><td>athletic</td></tr><tr><td>colour</td><td>colourful / coloured</td></tr></table>	1 mark for all 5 correct.	1 (G6.3)
43	Answers may vary, for example: The pair of dashes has been used to add extra information to the sentence. The pair of dashes has been used for parenthesis.	1 mark for answers that offer any valid explanation that refers to the use of dashes for parenthesis or to add extra information. Do not deduct marks for misspellings.	1 (G5.9)
44	If I were to go to Brazil, I would visit the rainforest.		1 (G4.3)
45	Answers may vary, for example: <table><tr><th>Noun</th><th>Noun phrase</th></tr><tr><td>the shed</td><td>the new shed in the garden</td></tr><tr><td>the bicycle</td><td>the shiny red bicycle over there</td></tr></table>	1 mark for any answer that creates a noun phrase by adding words both before and after the noun.	1 (G3.2)
46	Even though		1 (G3.4)
47	My cousins, Ana and Karl, who I know very well, live in Bath.		1 (G5.9)
48	<table><tr><th>Sentence</th><th>Noun phrase</th><th>Subordinate clause</th></tr><tr><td>I can't walk to school **because it's across town**.</td><td></td><td>✓</td></tr><tr><td>**Our family doctor** loves going fishing at the weekends.</td><td>✓</td><td></td></tr><tr><td>**After watching a show about them**, Ajay was amazed by sharks.</td><td></td><td>✓</td></tr></table>	1 mark for all 3 correct.	1 (G3.2 G3.4)

Grammar, Punctuation and Spelling Paper 2

Content Domain Coverage

Set A: Spelling

The table below shows the aspects of spelling assessed in Set A paper 2.

Qu.	Spelling	Content domain reference	Mark
1	distant	S55 — words ending in -ant, -ance, -ancy, -ent, -ence, -ency	1
2	mislay	S41 — prefixes	1
3	following	S38 — adding suffixes beginning with vowel letters to words of more than one syllable	1
4	usually	S43 — the suffix -ly	1
5	sensibly	S56 — words ending in -able and -ible, words ending in -ably and -ibly	1
6	meddle	S61 — homophones and near homophones	1
7	brilliant	S55 — words ending in -ant, -ance, -ancy, -ent, -ence, -ency	1
8	confident	S55 — words ending in -ant, -ance, -ancy, -ent, -ence, -ency	1
9	social	S54 — endings which sound like 'shul'	1
10	rough	S59 — words containing the letter string ough	1
11	interfering	S38 — adding suffixes beginning with vowel letters to words of more than one syllable	1
12	physical	S39 — the 'i' sound spelt y other than at the end of words	1
13	sacrifice	Years 5 and 6 word list	1
14	signature	S44 — words with endings sounding like 'zhuh' and 'chuh'	1
15	unique	S50 — words ending with the 'g' sound spelt -gue and the 'k' sound spelt -que	1
16	fascinate	S51 — words with the 's' sound spelt sc	1
17	ambitious	S53 — endings which sound like 'shus' spelt -cious or -tious	1
18	practise	S61 — homophones and near homophones	1
19	affects	S61 — homophones and near homophones	1
20	subtle	S60 — words with 'silent' letters	1

Set B: Spelling

The table below shows the aspects of spelling assessed in Set B paper 2.

Qu.	Spelling	Content domain reference	Mark
1	unable	S41 — prefixes	1
2	jealous	S46 — the suffix -ous	1
3	advice	S61 — homophones and near homophones	1
4	quarters	Years 3 and 4 word list	1
5	future	S44 — words with endings sounding like 'zhuh' and 'chuh'	1
6	vein	S52 — words with the 'ay' sound spelt ei, eigh, or ey	1
7	their	S61 — homophones and near homophones	1
8	echo	S48 — words with the 'k' sound spelt ch	1
9	trouble	S40 — the 'u' sound spelt ou	1
10	though	S59 — words containing the letter string ough	1
11	dictionary	Years 5 and 6 word list	1
12	thorough	S59 — words containing the letter string ough	1
13	whistle	S60 — words with 'silent' letters	1
14	disruption	S47 — endings that sound like 'shun', spelt -tion, -sion, -ssion, -cian	1
15	leisure	S44 — words with endings sounding like 'zhuh' and 'chuh'	1
16	transferred	S57 — adding suffixes beginning with vowel letters to words ending in –fer	1
17	celebration	S47 — endings that sound like 'shun', spelt -tion, -sion, -ssion, -cian	1
18	initials	S37 — common exception words	1
19	bruise	S60 — words with 'silent' letters	1
20	vicious	S53 — endings which sound like 'shus', spelt -cious or -tious	1

Guidance for Marking the Spelling Task

Here's some guidance for marking the paper 2 spelling tests:

- If the pupil makes more than one attempt, it needs to be clear which answer they wish to be marked. If the pupil makes two or more attempts and it isn't clear which is to be considered, the mark should not be awarded.
- Pupils can answer in lower or upper case, or a mixture of the two. This is not the case for days of the week and months of the year — these must be written in lower-case letters with an initial capital letter.
- If the pupil has answered with the correct sequence of letters but has incorrectly inserted an apostrophe or a hyphen, the mark should not be awarded.
- If the pupil has answered with the correct sequence of letters but these have been separated into clearly divided components, with or without a hyphen, the mark should not be awarded.

Instructions for the Spelling Task

Each test should take about 15 minutes to do. This isn't a strict limit, so you can allow more time if needed.

Read out the following instructions, and answer any questions the children may have.

> - *Listen to the instructions I'm about to give you.*
> - *I'm going to read out twenty sentences. These sentences are printed in your answer booklet, but each one has a word missing. Listen to the missing word and write it in. Make sure you spell it correctly.*
> - *I will read the word, then read the word within a sentence, then I'll say the word a third time.*
> - *Have you got any questions?*

Now read the spellings to the children:

> - Say the spelling number
> - Say *"The word is..."*
> - Read out the word in its sentence.
> - Say *"The word is..."*
> - Pause for at least 12 seconds between each of the spellings.

At the end of the test, read out all 20 sentences again, and give the children time to change their answers if they want to.

When the test is over, say "This is the end of the test."

Set A: Spelling – Script

Spelling one — the word is **distant**. *The King of Spain is my **distant** relative.* The word is **distant**.

Spelling two — the word is **mislay**. *Be careful not to **mislay** your tickets.* The word is **mislay**.

Spelling three — the word is **following**. *Kate is driving, and Kofi is **following** her on his bike.* The word is **following**.

Spelling four — the word is **usually**. *The door is **usually** left unlocked.* The word is **usually**.

Spelling five — the word is **sensibly**. *They acted **sensibly** to make a good impression.* The word is **sensibly**.

Spelling six — the word is **meddle**. *Karine likes to **meddle** in other people's business.* The word is **meddle**.

Spelling seven — the word is **brilliant**. *Siân makes **brilliant** cupcakes and biscuits.* The word is **brilliant**.

Spelling eight — the word is **confident**. *The dancers felt more **confident** after the rehearsal.* The word is **confident**.

Spelling nine — the word is **social**. *Many animals live in **social** groups.* The word is **social**.

Spelling ten — the word is **rough**. *Toads have **rough** skin.* The word is **rough**.

Spelling eleven — the word is **interfering**. *The storm is **interfering** with my radio.* The word is **interfering**.

Spelling twelve — the word is **physical**. *We had a **physical** examination before the dive trip.* The word is **physical**.

Spelling thirteen — the word is **sacrifice**. *He had to **sacrifice** a lot of free time to become a sprinter.* The word is **sacrifice**.

Spelling fourteen — the word is **signature**. *My mum's **signature** just looks like a scribble.* The word is **signature**.

Spelling fifteen — the word is **unique**. *The **unique** statue sold for a lot of money.* The word is **unique**.

Spelling sixteen — the word is **fascinate**. *Joe used to **fascinate** the children with his juggling.* The word is **fascinate**.

Spelling seventeen — the word is **ambitious**. *She is the most **ambitious** person that I know.* The word is **ambitious**.

Spelling eighteen — the word is **practise**. *You need to **practise** spelling tricky words.* The word is **practise**.

Spelling nineteen — the word is **affects**. *The weather always **affects** my mood.* The word is **affects**.

Spelling twenty — the word is **subtle**. *There is a **subtle** difference between the colours.* The word is **subtle**.

Set B: Spelling – Script

Spelling one — the word is **unable**. *I was so shocked that I was **unable** to speak.* The word is **unable**.

Spelling two — the word is **jealous**. *Maya is very **jealous** of Sami's birthday present.* The word is **jealous**.

Spelling three — the word is **advice**. *The man wanted the hairdresser's **advice**.* The word is **advice**.

Spelling four — the word is **quarters**. *We cut the pizza into **quarters**.* The word is **quarters**.

Spelling five — the word is **future**. *In the **future**, she wants to travel to the moon.* The word is **future**.

Spelling six — the word is **vein**. *The doctor looked for a **vein** to give Martha her injection.* The word is **vein**.

Spelling seven — the word is **their**. *The children loved **their** new toys.* The word is **their**.

Spelling eight — the word is **echo**. *If you shout in a cave, the sound will **echo**.* The word is **echo**.

Spelling nine — the word is **trouble**. *His mother told him to keep out of **trouble**.* The word is **trouble**.

Spelling ten — the word is **though**. *Even **though** he was tired, he kept going.* The word is **though**.

Spelling eleven — the word is **dictionary**. *Jim found the word in the class **dictionary**.* The word is **dictionary**.

Spelling twelve — the word is **thorough**. *Dad asked me to give the car a **thorough** clean.* The word is **thorough**.

Spelling thirteen — the word is **whistle**. *Mum likes to **whistle** as she mows the lawn.* The word is **whistle**.

Spelling fourteen — the word is **disruption**. *Bring a Pet to School Day always causes **disruption**.* The word is **disruption**.

Spelling fifteen — the word is **leisure**. *They will spend the day at the **leisure** centre.* The word is **leisure**.

Spelling sixteen — the word is **transferred**. *Lena **transferred** the boxes from the car to the shed.* The word is **transferred**.

Spelling seventeen — the word is **celebration**. *There was a big **celebration** when the team won.* The word is **celebration**.

Spelling eighteen — the word is **initials**. *I wrote my **initials** on all of my books.* The word is **initials**.

Spelling nineteen — the word is **bruise**. *She fell off the swing and has a **bruise** on her leg.* The word is **bruise**.

Spelling twenty — the word is **vicious**. *Seagulls are **vicious** if they want your chips.* The word is **vicious**.

KS2 English
SATS Practice Papers

This brilliant pack from CGP is filled with the most realistic SATs practice you'll find, all fully up to date for the latest tests!

It contains two full sets of English Practice Papers, carefully crafted to be just like the real tests. We've also included full answers and mark schemes.

In case that wasn't enough, we've also thrown in some free online extras — including a Parents' Guide, pupil-friendly answers, quizzes and more!

How to access your free Online Extras

This pack includes free Online Extras to access on your PC, Mac or tablet. You'll just need to go to **cgpbooks.co.uk/extras** and enter this code:

2370 8692 2976 1989

By the way, this code only works for one person. If somebody else has used this book before you, they might have already claimed the Online Extras.

What CGP is all about

Our sole aim here at CGP is to produce the highest quality books — carefully written, immaculately presented and dangerously close to being funny.

Then we work our socks off to get them out to you — at the cheapest possible prices.